# YOUR
# QUESTIONS
## ANSWERED

## —A REPLY TO
## MUSLIM FRIENDS

E. M. Hicham

**EP BOOKS** (Evangelical Press)
Unit C, Tomlinson Road, Leyland, PR25 2DY

epbooks@100fthose.com

www.epbooks.org

First published 2008
Reprinted 2009 Second
impression 2012 Third
impression 2014 This
edition 2016

British Library Cataloguing in Publication Data available

ISBN: 978-0-85234-694-5

# Contents

# How to read Bible references

Matthew 24:35 = The Gospel of Matthew,
chapter 24, verse 35

# Introduction

## 'Assalamou Alaikoum'

THESE WERE THE WORDS JESUS USED TO GREET HIS DISCIPLES. They mean, 'Peace to you.' In fact his purpose in coming to this world was to bring us peace *with* God and the peace *of* God. One of the prophets called Jesus 'the Prince of Peace'. Jesus was a peacemaker, and he taught his followers to act in the same way. They must be at peace with others and should show love, not only to those closest to them, such as their families and other Christians, but also to their neighbour—that is, everyone they meet. Jesus even taught that his followers should love those who disagree with them!

So it is with a spirit of love and respect that I write this book. I write not as someone cleverer or more intellectual than you, but only as someone whom God pitied; whose eyes God has opened to see the wonder of the truths contained in his Holy Word. I had rejected the Bible for years. In fact, I hated everything to do with Christianity. I was taught that the Bible had been changed and therefore there was no need for me even to pick it up. But God had mercy on me. One day I was given an Arabic Injil (New Testament). I said to myself, 'Why can't I read this book? Even the Qur'an recommends it to me. Let me read it and see what the people of the book (Christians) believe.'

And so, with many presuppositions, such as, 'The Bible has been changed', 'Christians worship three gods', 'God could never have a son', 'The immorality of Western society is caused by Christianity', I started studying the Injil. Later I was surprised to learn that Christians also have the Tawrat (the Pentateuch) and Zabur (the Psalms) in their Bible! They have all of God's Holy Scriptures. This was a major discovery for me.

As I meet with Muslims I find that they often have many misunderstandings about the Christian faith. They are asking questions similar to those that I had. It is such questions that I want to address and answer in this book. I am aware that many Muslims ask and discuss with an open mind. You may be one of them. If you are sincerely seeking the truth, then to you I address this small work.

My prayer is that God will be glorified as you read on. I give praise to our loving, holy, just, gracious and merciful God, of whom this book endeavours to speak. God alone is worthy, and so to him be all praise and worship, both now and for ever.

# 1
## What is the Bible?

THROUGHOUT THE AGES, GOD HAS GIVEN INSTRUCTIONS TO MAN concerning how he should live and how to find the way to paradise.

The word 'Bible' is of Greek origin and simply means *the book*. It is a collection of sixty-six books written by about forty authors, in three different languages, over approximately 1600 years (between 1500 BC and AD 100). It is the most widely circulated book of all time, and it has now been translated, in whole or in part, into well over 2000 languages and dialects.

The Bible is inspired and without error. God spoke through his Holy Spirit to men, and they wrote as the Holy Spirit breathed upon them. The Bible says, 'No prophecy of Scripture is of any private interpretation, for prophecy never came by the will of man, but holy men of God spoke as they were moved by the Holy Spirit' (Injil, 2 Peter 1:20–21). The apostle Paul said, 'All Scripture is given by inspiration of God, and is profitable for doctrine, for reproof, for correction, for instruction in righteousness' (Injil, 2 Timothy 3:16). This means that the Bible is the Word of God and it is without error in every subject it addresses.

The Bible contains many different styles of writing, such as poetry, narration, history, law and prophecy. It is the foundation of the Christian faith, and teaches the Christian how to apply God's Word to his life. It is divided into two major sections: the Old Testament, written before the birth of Jesus Christ in Hebrew (with a few passages in Aramaic); and the New Testament, written in Greek in the first century after Jesus died.

## The Old Testament books

These were written by prophets such as Moses, David and Isaiah. There are thirty-nine books:

**Torah (Tawrat)**—5 books of Moses:
Genesis, Exodus, Leviticus, Numbers, Deuteronomy.

**Historical**—12 books:
Joshua, Judges, Ruth, 1 Samuel, 2 Samuel, 1 Kings, 2 Kings, 1 Chronicles, 2 Chronicles, Ezra, Nehemiah, Esther.

**Poetical**—5 books:
Job, Psalms (Zabur), Proverbs, Ecclesiastes, Song of Solomon.

**Prophetical**—17 books:
*Major Prophets*—Isaiah, Jeremiah, Lamentations, Ezekiel, Daniel;
*Minor Prophets*—Hosea, Joel, Amos, Obadiah, Jonah, Micah, Nahum, Habakkuk, Zephaniah, Haggai, Zechariah, Malachi.

## The New Testament books

The second part of the Bible is often known as the gospel, a word taken from Greek which literally means *good news*. In the singular (the gospel), it refers to the message of Jesus Christ. However, the plural (the Gospels) is used to indicate the four books which give accounts of Jesus' life on earth. Thus the gospel of Jesus is told in the four Gospels of Matthew, Mark, Luke and John, as well as in the rest of the New Testament writings.

The New Testament contains twenty-seven books that were written in Greek by people who either knew Jesus or who were under the guidance of those who did. They are listed as follows:

**The Gospels**—4 books:
Matthew, Mark, Luke, John.

**The Acts of the Apostles**
Written by Luke, it describes the early Christians and the beginning of the church.

**The letters written by the apostle Paul**—13 books: Romans, 1 Corinthians, 2 Corinthians, Galatians, Ephesians, Philippians, Colossians, 1 Thessalonians, 2 Thessalonians, 1 Timothy, 2 Timothy, Titus, Philemon.

**Other letters**—8 books:
Hebrews, James, 1 Peter, 2 Peter, 1 John, 2 John, 3 John, Jude.

**Revelation**
This was written by one of Jesus' disciples, John (the same John who wrote one of the Gospels). It is the last book of the Bible, and recounts a vision given by Jesus to John. It describes the opposition and sufferings that Christians will meet and encourages them to keep their hope alive, by fixing their eyes upon what will take place at the return of Jesus Christ.

### The overall message of the Bible

The Bible starts by addressing the question, 'Where do we come from?' and ends with, 'Where are we going?' It describes the origin of man in the Garden of Eden, along with his fall into sin and out of fellowship with God. It then describes how God, through Abraham, called out to himself a special people, the Israelites. He promised that out of this people would come a future Messiah, a Saviour who would restore mankind's relationship with God.

The Bible is the account of the work of God in history, bringing to fruition his prophetic declarations concerning Jesus Christ. Jesus was born of a virgin. He died on the cross, bearing the punishment that our sins deserve, just as was promised in the Old Testament. For example, seven hundred years before the birth of Jesus, a prophet called Isaiah foretold what the coming Messiah would do and why he would come. 'Surely he [Jesus] has borne our griefs and carried our sorrows; yet we esteemed him stricken, smitten by God, and afflicted. But he was wounded for our transgressions, he was bruised for our iniquities; the chastisement for our peace was upon him, and by his stripes we are healed. All we like sheep have gone astray; we have turned, every one, to his own way; and the LORD has laid on him the iniquity of us all. He was oppressed and he was afflicted, yet he opened not his mouth; he was led as a lamb to the slaughter, and as a sheep before its shearers is silent, so he opened not his mouth ... And they made his grave with the wicked—but with the rich at his death, because he had done no violence, nor was any deceit in his mouth' (Isaiah 53:4–9).

Describing his mission, Jesus himself said to his disciples: '"These are the words which I spoke to you while I was still with you, that all things must be fulfilled which were written in the Law of Moses and the Prophets and the Psalms concerning me." And he opened their understanding, that they might comprehend the Scriptures. Then he said to them, "Thus it is written, and thus it was necessary for the Christ to suffer and to rise from the dead the third day, and that repentance and remission of sins should be preached in his name to all nations, beginning at Jerusalem' (Luke 24:44–47).

Just as Isaiah prophesied, Jesus lived a perfect, sinless life. He remained silent when he was falsely accused. He died amongst wicked people; crucified between two criminals. He was buried in a rich man's tomb. All this took place, as Isaiah foretold, because of our wickedness. After Jesus' death, the apostle Peter wrote to Christians, saying that Jesus, 'bore our sins in his own body on the tree, that we, having died to sins, might live for righteousness—by whose stripes you were healed. For you were like sheep going astray, but have now returned to the Shepherd and Overseer of your souls' (1 Peter 2:24–25).

Jesus didn't stay dead. He rose from the dead. He is alive and one day he will return as the great Judge. He will reward those who trust in him and will punish those who reject his offer of salvation. Both the Old and New Testaments focus on the person and work of Jesus Christ, the Messiah.

The following anonymous paragraph summarizes well what the followers of Jesus believe about the Holy Bible:

> This book contains the mind of God, the state of man, the way of salvation, the doom of sinners and the happiness of believers. Its doctrines are holy, its precepts are binding, its histories are true and its decisions are immutable. Read it to be wise, believe it to be saved and practise it to be holy. It contains light to direct you, food to support you and comfort to cheer you. It is the traveller's map, the pilot's compass, the soldier's sword and the Christian's charter. Here paradise is restored, Heaven opened, and the gates of hell disclosed. Christ is its grand subject, our good its design, and the glory of God its end. Read it slowly, frequently, prayerfully. It is a mine of wealth, a paradise of glory ... It will reward the greatest labour and condemn all who trifle with its sacred contents. It is the Book of books—God's book—the revelation of God to man.[1]

## Note

1. Quoted by S. Olyott, *You Might Have Asked*, Evangelical Press, 1983, p.14.

# 2

# Has the Bible been changed?

I OFTEN HEAR THIS QUESTION. MANY PEOPLE ARE TAUGHT THAT THE Christian Scriptures have been changed. But have you thought about how serious this claim is? What they are attacking is the Word of God revealed in the Tawrat, Zabur and Injil. The Holy Bible that the followers of Jesus have today is the same as the original Bible. It could not have been corrupted. Consider the following facts

## God's severe warning

Christians love their Holy Scriptures and would never let anyone change them. The Bible warns that those who try to change God's Word will be severely punished. A long time ago God spoke through Moses (in the Tawrat) commanding, 'You shall not add to the word which I command you, nor take from it, that you may keep the commandments of the LORD your God which I command you' (Deuteronomy 4:2).

Four centuries later Solomon (سليمان) said, 'Every word of God is pure; he is a shield to those who put their trust in him. Do not add to his words, lest he rebuke you, and you be found a liar' (Proverbs 30:5–6)

Even when the last book of the Bible was written, God said through the apostle John, 'For I testify to everyone who hears the words of the prophecy of this book: If anyone adds to these things, God will add to him the plagues that are written in this book; and if anyone takes away from the words of the book of this prophecy, God shall take away his part from the Book of Life, from the holy city, and from the things which are written in this book' (Revelation 22:18–19).

These warnings are clear. No believer would dare to change God's Word.

## The number of Bibles

Imagine that copies of a book written by a Mr Abdel Aziz were given to every family in your town, including your own family. All the copies were the same and each copy was a perfect reproduction of the original book. Later, someone suddenly said that the book had been changed and could no longer be trusted. Would you have accepted that claim when you had a reliable copy in your hands? Surely you would have said, 'Wait a minute, I've got a copy of the original book at home and it hasn't been changed.' Others would bring out their perfect copies too.

So it was with the Bible. The original manuscripts were reproduced very carefully. Whenever a new copy was made, it was strictly checked. Many reproductions of the original manuscripts existed. If someone had wanted to change the Bible they would have had to gather all the reproductions from each house—from Europe, Africa, the Middle East—and then change them. Is that possible? No! Even if one copy had been changed, those people who owned the true copies would have noticed and condemned it.

## Muslim scholars and the Qur'an

No one attacked or questioned the genuineness of the Bible until AD 1046 (over 400 years after Muhammad died). In 1046 Ibn-Hazm (who died at Cordoba in AD 1064) first made the charge that the Bible had been corrupted and falsified. Ibn-Hazm's aim was to defend

Islam against Christianity because he had come upon differences and contradictions between the Bible and the Qur'an. Believing by faith that the Qur'an was true, the Bible must then be false. He said, 'Since the Qur'an must be true it must be the conflicting Gospel texts that are false. But Muhammad tells us to respect the Gospel. Therefore, the present text must have been falsified by the Christians after the time of Muhammad.'

His argument was not based on any evidence or historical facts but only on his personal faith; his desire to safeguard the Qur'an.[1] 'If we prove the falsehood of their books, they lose the arguments they take from them.'[2] This led him to teach that 'The Christians lost the revealed Gospel except for a few traces which God has left intact as argument against them.'[3]

Muhammad believed that the Bible which existed in his day was authentic (read Surahs 5:68–69; 3:3; 21:7; 21:48–50; 4:162–163; 35:31; 9:111; 6:154–157; 40:69–70; 46:12; 46:29–30). Early scholars of Islam and many others after them refused to believe that the Tawrat, Zabur and Injil had been changed. According to many scholars, the Qur'an says the Scriptures were *misrepresented*, not that they were changed.

Commenting on Surah 2:75, Imam Baydaoui says, 'Can ye entertain the hope that they (that is, Jews) will believe in you?—Seeing that a party of them heard the word of Allah and perverted it knowingly … *meaning they misinterpreted and explained it as they like* … after they understood it.'

يقول الإمام البيضاوي: "أفتطمعون أن يصدقونكم (أي اليهود) وقد كانت طائفة من أسلافهم يسمعون كلام الله أي التوراة ثم يحرفونه ...أي يؤولونه ويفسرونه بما يشتهون...من بعد ما عقلوه أي فهموه بعقولهم ولم يبق فيه ريبة."

In his commentary, Imam Bukhari explains Surah 4:46 as follows: 'displace words from their right places … means misinterpreted.

ويقول <u>صحيح البخاري</u>: "يحرفون الكلم عن موضعه أي يزيلونه وليس أحد يزيل لفظ كتاب من كتب الله تعالى، ولكنهم يؤولونه على غير تأويله".

You can also read similar comments made by Imam Razi.

Some people who called themselves 'Christians' in Muhammad's time had stopped reading God's Word. Instead, they followed traditions created by men. It is true that they had 'misinterpreted' God's Word. But the Holy Scriptures themselves had not been changed. They had been forgotten. Throughout history, however, there have been true Christians who have loved, protected and followed God's Word.

## The number of ancient manuscripts

If early Muslim scholars thought the Bible that existed in their time was genuine, then any document from before the seventh century must be authentic. Manuscripts of the Tawrat, Zabur and Injil (the Old and New Testaments), dating back to several hundred years before the rise of Islam, are displayed in well-known museums across the world. The Vatican and Sinaitic manuscripts date from only two centuries after the completion of the Bible. Anyone can compare them with the Bible that we have today and see that it has not been corrupted. There are also many other ancient manuscripts which contain quotations from the Bible, or part of the Bible. These all confirm the integrity of the text Christians use to this day.

I ask you, then, to answer this question: When was the Bible changed? Before or after Muhammad? If it was changed beforehand you are accusing Muhammad of being a false teacher. On the other hand, it could not have been changed afterwards because by then the Bible had been translated into many languages and widely distributed across the world.

## The unity of the message

The Bible has one great story running from beginning to end.

Throughout the long period of history that it covers, there are no contradictions. God's great plan is always central. This is why the Bible is amazing and unique! The Tawrat, the Zabur and the Injil are all about Christ and how God planned to deal with our problem of sin. All the prophets of the Old Testament talked about the Messiah, the Saviour who would come to offer himself and save sinners. The New Testament talks about the fact that that promised Saviour has come. It shows that he was none other than Jesus.

If someone had changed part of the Bible, surely certain sections would contradict others. They do not. There is a clear unity of thought between all sections of the Bible. Muslim writers cling to a few parallel passages where they assume there are contradictions in various numbers and ages. In doing this, several verses are often referenced as being problematic. With an earnest and genuine study, one can be sure that those assumptions are absolutely untrue. We can trust the Bible to be what it says it is: the Word of God.[4]

### God guards his Word

The Bible is the Word of God. God who created everything, the Almighty, who knows everything, is the Author of the Bible. Because he is God, he is able to protect his Word from corruption and change. Here is what he says in the Zabur, 'Forever O LORD, your Word is settled in heaven' (Psalm 119:89). The Injil says, 'Heaven and earth will pass away, but my words will by no means pass away' (Matthew 24:35). God's Holy Word is eternal. It stands for ever. He would never permit his everlasting Word to be changed. God has kept this promise throughout the centuries. It is unthinkable to imagine that a feeble human being could change the very word spoken by God. It is blasphemy to say that the Bible has been changed because by saying this, you accuse God of two things. First, that God is a liar for not keeping his promise; and second, that God is not God since he was unable to keep his Holy Word. If the Bible has been changed, then God was not able to protect it. It would mean that man is greater than

God. And, my friend, if God was not able to protect his Word, then he is not God! That is blasphemy.

## What about different translations?

As mentioned in the first chapter of this book, the original Bible was written in Hebrew, Greek and Aramaic. Many manuscripts of the Holy Bible still exist in these languages. However, God wanted everyone in the world to be able to read his Word. In order to make this possible the Bible has been translated into different languages. This does not mean that these Bibles are corrupted, but it does mean that there are many translations *of* the Bible. For example, in English we have the King James Version which was translated back in AD 1611 and which is still widely used today. However, since then, the language of the people has developed and changed, so the translations have been updated to make the Holy Bible more readable. Since these translations are made from very old documents, there is no difference in their meaning. Every translation must agree with the ancient manuscripts. If it does not, it is not accepted. The version offered by the Jehovah's Witnesses, for example, is not an accurate translation of those documents. That is why Christians everywhere strictly condemn what they have done. One day God will judge them for it.

## Where are the original Tawrat and Injil?

The Qur'an states that the Tawrat, Zabur and Injil were sent down to Moses, David and Jesus by dictation. It also teaches that they were very similar to the Qur'an (Qur'an, Surah 3:3, Yusuf Ali translation). So Muslims look for the actual gospel that was with God in heaven and which was revealed to Jesus. They often say, 'The Bible you have today is not the original Tawrat and Injil which were revealed to Moses and Jesus respectively. You have the books of Paul and other writers but not the Word of God.'

There is no historical evidence whatsoever that books revealed to Moses and Jesus, in the form of the Qur'an, ever existed. Not so much as a page can be found anywhere to support the Muslim claim that these were the original scriptures. This teaching of the Qur'an has no support at all in the factual records of human history.

The problem for Muslims is that the only two books the Jews and Christians have ever known as their holy scriptures are the Old and New Testaments. They are consistent with one another and the latter consistently quotes from the former. Each contains narrative works, prophetic material, quotations from prophets and apostles, the actual words of God and instructive teaching. Neither, however, is remotely like the Qur'an.

Since the books that the Christians and Jews have always had are so different to any 'Tawrat' and 'Injil' in the form described by the Qur'an, the real task before Muslims is to produce the original books or at least some evidence of their former state. Until they do so, it can only be presumed that such books never existed.

## What is your answer?

The Bible is a message from God to sinful people. In it, God is calling us to have a relationship with himself. But how is it possible for me, a sinner, to come close to the holy God? In the Bible, God reveals to us his plan of salvation. That is why Christians believe that there is no power that can change God's Word.

It is a serious thing to say that God's Holy Scriptures have been changed! This claim cannot be supported by facts

However, if the Bible we have today is true, then we should not ignore it. Each of us must read and obey God's Holy Scriptures, accepting them as his pure word, 'which is able to save your souls' (James 1:21). In accepting the Tawrat, Zabur and Injil as the holy word of God, we must also accept their unchanging message. This message is that, though we are sinners (those who have disobeyed God in our thoughts, words and actions), God has provided a solution. He sent Jesus as our Substitute. Jesus our Saviour lived the perfect life that we should have lived, and then he died the death that we deserve to die. He died to bear the punishment for our wrongdoing. His death satisfied the justice and love of God. By trusting in what Jesus has done for us, we can know that our sins have been forgiven. Our relationship with our Creator will be restored. God will give us a new heart and help us to live increasingly as we ought to live.

> From childhood you have known the Holy Scriptures, which are able to make you wise for salvation through faith which is in Christ Jesus
> (Injil, 2 Timothy 3:15).

## Notes

1. I. Di Matteo, 'Il "takhrif" od alterazione della Bibbia secondo i musulmani', Bessarione 38 (1922) 64–111; 223–260; 'Le preteze contradizzioni della S. Scrittura secondo Ibn-Hazm', Bessarione 39 (1923) 77–127, E. Fritsch, *op. cit.*, p. 66.

2. Ibn-Hazm, Kitab al-fasl fi'l-milah wa'l ahwa'l nikhal, II,6; E. Fritsch, *op. cit.*, p.55.

3. Ibn-Hazm, *ibid.*; E. Fritsch, *op. cit.*, p. 64.

4. For more details read *Nothing but the truth*, by Brian Edwards; and *Why believe the Bible?* by John Blanchard. Both of these books are published by Evangelical Press.

# 3
# Why have Christians hidden
# the 'Gospel of Barnabas'?

I WELL REMEMBER ONE OF MY FIRST CONVERSATIONS WITH A Muslim. This is what he said:

The Church has hidden the 'Gospel of Barnabas'! It was part of the Injil until the Council of Nicea in AD 325. But since then the church has suppressed it! If you read it you'll see that Jesus foretold the coming of Muhammad. It is the only true record of the life of Jesus Christ. Christians have hidden the 'Gospel of Barnabas' because it shows that Jesus was the prophet Islam declares him to be.

Maybe you have heard or said something like this yourself? I had never heard of the 'Gospel of Barnabas' so I couldn't answer my Muslim friend. 'You see,' he said, 'your ignorance of it proves that the Church has suppressed it.'

I wanted to know whether or not this 'Gospel' was reliable, so I found a copy and began to study it. Here is a summary of what I discovered.

## The history of the 'Barnabas Gospel'

In 1734 George Sale published an English translation of the Qur'an. He mentioned a 'Gospel of Barnabas' in the introduction. Sale said there was a Spanish translation (which no longer exists apart from a few known extracts), and an Italian translation which was kept in the library of Prince Eugene of Savoy.

The preface of the Italian version said that a Roman Catholic monk, Fra Marino (1590), found the 'Gospel of Barnabas' in the library of Pope Sixtus V. The monk quickly took the book, read it and converted to Islam.

Sale wrote that the 'Gospel of Barnabas' records the life of Jesus very differently from the four biblical Gospels. It corresponds to the Qur'an and Hadith in several ways:

- Jesus' denial that he was the Son of God (Gospel of Barnabas, para. 70);
- Judas crucified in place of Jesus (Gospel of Barnabas, para. 116);
- Jesus predicting the coming of Muhammad (Gospel of Barnabas, para. 112).

Sale did not think the book was a genuine Gospel.

In 1907, Lonsdale and Laura Ragg published an English translation of the 'Gospel of Barnabas'. They also said they thought the 'Gospel' was fake. Their translation was first published in the Muslim world in 1973. It is estimated that, since then, about 100,000 copies have been printed in Pakistan alone. Translations into Arabic and other languages were also published. These materials caused excitement among Muslims. They thought they had at last found a document—of Christian origin—which proved that Jesus was the Isa Al-Massih of Islam and that Muhammad was the predicted messenger of Allah.

## Evidences against the authenticity of the 'Barnabas Gospel'

Most Muslims believe that this 'Gospel' is rejected by Christians only because of its Islamic character. However, there are many internal and external factors which provide far better grounds for rejecting it.

### Barnabas could never have been its author

Muslims say that the 'Gospel of Barnabas' is an original Gospel, written in the first century AD by a Jewish man who travelled with Jesus.

The book claims to have been written by one of the twelve disciples of Jesus. The biblical Barnabas, however, only appeared on the scene after Jesus' death and resurrection. We read in the Bible:

> And Joses, who was also named Barnabas by the apostles (which is translated Son of Encouragement), a Levite of the country of Cyprus, having land, sold it, and brought the money and laid it at the apostles' feet                                   (Injil, Acts 4:36–37).

This man Joses was given the name Barnabas by the apostles. He was certainly not one of the original twelve disciples, whose names are mentioned in two of the Gospels (Matthew 10:2–4; and Luke 6:14–16). Barnabas is not in either list, nor does his name appear anywhere in all four Gospels. This fact is plainly contradicted in the 'Gospel of Barnabas'. It says that Jesus called Barnabas by name on several occasions, for example, 'Jesus answered: "Be not sore grieved, Barnabas, for those whom God chose before the creation of the world shall not perish"' (Gospel of Barnabas, para. 19). Jesus could not have said these words to Barnabas, since Barnabas received his name sometime after Jesus went up to heaven! There is further evidence that this book was not written by Barnabas.

### Its linguistic, historical and geographical errors

If Barnabas really was the author, he would have been familiar with the basic facts of Jewish life at this time. Let us see if the author was.

*a. Christ.* The word χριστός (Christ) is the Greek translation for the Hebrew word מָשִׁיחַ (Messiah). When translated into English both these words mean *the Anointed One* or *the Chosen One*. This word is not rare. It is one of the most common words in Jewish and Christian vocabulary. There is no doubt that a religious Jew like the biblical Barnabas would have been familiar with it.

At the very start of the 'Gospel of Barnabas' Jesus is called the Christ: 'God has during these past days visited us by his prophet Jesus *Christ*' (para. 2). Throughout the book, however, Jesus denies being the Messiah: 'Jesus confessed and said the truth, "I am not the *Messiah*"' (para. 42). How could Jesus be the Christ and yet deny being the Messiah, when both words mean exactly the same thing? Whoever wrote this book did not know that the Greek meaning of the word Christ is *Messiah*. The real Barnabas was Hebrew, he knew Greek, and could not have made this mistake.

*b. The rulers of the first century AD.* In paragraph 3 of the book we are told that Herod and Pilate both ruled in Judea at the time of Jesus' birth: 'There reigned at that time in Judea Herod, by decree of Caesar Augustus, and Pilate was governor.' This is historically wrong. Pilate was not governor when Jesus was born. The governor at that time was King Herod who ruled alone from 37–4 BC.[1] Pilate ruled thirty years later from AD 26–36. King Herod and Pilate never ruled in Judea at the same time. This has been affirmed historically.

The real Barnabas lived during the rule of Pilate, so if he was the writer of this book, how could he make such a simple mistake?

*c. Geography.* In paragraphs 20–21 we are told about Jesus sailing to Nazareth and being welcomed by the seamen of that town. He then leaves Nazareth and goes up to Capernaum:

> Jesus went to the sea of Galilee, and having embarked in a ship sailed to his city of Nazareth ... Having arrived at the city of Nazareth the seamen spread through the city all that Jesus wrought [did] ... (then) Jesus went up to Capernaum.

Jesus often visited Nazareth and Capernaum with his disciples, so they must have known these towns well. The author of this book, however, did not! Nazareth was not a fishing village. In fact it was about fourteen kilometres from the sea of Galilee, situated in the foothills of a mountain range! Capernaum was the fishing village Jesus arrived at with his disciples, not Nazareth. The author could not have been a disciple of Jesus. This mistake also makes us doubt that he had ever lived in that region.

What can we conclude from this? The 'Gospel of Barnabas' makes basic mistakes about the language, history and geography of the Jewish world in the first century AD. These mistakes suggest that it was not written by Barnabas in the first century.

### Its medieval date

There are many proofs that the 'Gospel of Barnabas' is a fifteenth-century forgery. As mentioned above, the introductory notes of the Raggs' translation stated that it was a medieval fabrication. They believed it to be the work of an apostate from Christianity, dating from sometime between the thirteenth and sixteenth centuries.

Mr Khalil Saada, who translated the Barnabas 'Gospel' into Arabic in 1908, wrote in his introduction: 'All the historians agree that Barnabas' Bible was written in the intermediary ages.' Surprisingly, these introductory notes were omitted from later publications.

It is not difficult to prove that this 'Gospel' was first compiled centuries after the times of both Jesus and Muhammad. Consider the following facts:

*a. The manuscript evidence.* The oldest copies are written in Italian and Spanish. These date from the fifteenth century or later.

*b. The jubilee year.* In the time of Moses God told the Jews to observe a Jubilee year every fifty years:

> And you shall consecrate the fiftieth year, and proclaim liberty throughout all the land to all its inhabitants. It shall be a Jubilee for you; and each of you shall return to his possession, and each of you shall

return to his family. That fiftieth year shall be a Jubilee to you; in it you shall neither sow nor reap what grows of its own accord, nor gather the grapes of your untended vine                    (Leviticus 25:10–11).

In the year 1300 Pope Boniface VIII wrongly declared that the Jubilee should be celebrated every hundred years. After his death, the next pope, Clement VI, changed it back to every fifty years. Therefore, in church history there was a specific period of time when the Jubilee was thought by many to be every hundred years. In the 'Gospel of Barnabas' these words are put on Jesus' lips: 'Insomuch that the year of Jubilee, which now comes every 100 years, shall by the Messiah be reduced to every year in every place' (para. 82).

The author of the 'Gospel of Barnabas' unwittingly accepted the pope's false decree and included it in his book! He must have lived during or after the time of Pope Boniface VIII.

Is there further evidence to suggest that the 'Gospel of Barnabas' dates from the fourteenth or fifteenth century? Yes, there is.

*c. Quotations from Dante.* Dante was a famous and popular poet of the fourteenth century who lived at about the same time as Pope Boniface. Among Dante's works is a book of poetry called *The Divine Comedy*. In this book he describes ascending through nine heavens to reach paradise, the tenth. Many passages in the 'Gospel of Barnabas' show a dependence on Dante's work. For example, like Dante, the author speaks of nine heavens and says that paradise is greater than all of them put together:

> Paradise is so great that no man can measure it. Verily I say unto thee that the heavens are *nine*, among which are set the planets, that are distant one from another five hundred years journey for a man ... and Verily I say unto thee that paradise is greater than all the earth and heavens together (para. 178).

It appears that the author of the 'Gospel of Barnabas' took the idea of nine heavens from reading Dante.

*d. Wine barrels.* The 'Gospel of Barnabas' speaks of storing wine in wooden wine-casks (para. 152). This was a common practice in medieval Europe but not in first-century Palestine where wine was stored in skins (Matthew 9:17). Once again, this shows that the author was more at home in medieval Europe than in the land of Palestine.

## How the 'Gospel of Barnabas' contradicts the teachings of Islam

Though the 'Gospel of Barnabas' supports the teachings of Islam in many ways, there are a few occasions when it does not.

*a. The Messiah—Jesus or Muhammad?* In John 1:20 (Injil), John the Baptist denies that he is the Messiah. The 'Gospel of Barnabas', however, makes Jesus deny the same thing in much the same words:

> Jesus confessed and said the truth, 'I am not the Messiah ... I am indeed sent to the house of Israel as a prophet of salvation; but after me shall come the Messiah' (paras 42, 82).

> Then said the priest: 'How shall the Messiah be called?' ... [Jesus answered] 'Muhammad is his blessed name' (para. 97).

Here the author of the 'Gospel of Barnabas' trips himself up, since the Qur'an (like the Bible) teaches that Jesus alone *is* the Messiah, and it *never* teaches that Muhammad is the Messiah: 'O Mary! Allah giveth thee glad tidings of a word from him, His name will be Christ Jesus, the son of Mary' (Surah 3:45, Yusuf Ali translation).

*b. The birth of Jesus.* The Qur'an says that Mary had pain when she gave birth to Jesus: 'So she conceived him, and she retired with him to a remote place. And *the pains of childbirth* drove her to the trunk of a palm tree' (Surah 19:22–23, Yusuf Ali).

However, the 'Gospel of Barnabas' teaches the opposite: 'The virgin was surrounded by a light exceeding bright, and brought forth her son *without pain*' (para. 3). This statement contradicts both the Bible and the Qur'an. It also proves the 'Gospel's' fifteenth-century origin, since it parallels Catholic beliefs of the Middle Ages.

*c. The heavens.* The Qur'an says that there are seven heavens: 'The seven heavens and the earth, and all beings therein, declare His glory' (Surah 17:44, Yusuf Ali). The 'Gospel of Barnabas', however, teaches that there are nine: 'Verily I say unto thee that the heavens are nine, among which are set the planets, that are distant one from another five hundred years journey for a man' (para. 178).

*d. The last days.* While the Qur'an states that men will be alive until the Day of Judgement, when the trumpet shall sound (Surah 80:37), the 'Gospel of Barnabas' says that on the thirteenth day of the final period before the end, all mankind will die and every living thing in earth shall perish (para. 53).

*e. Death of angels.* The author of the Barnabas 'Gospel' wrote that during the last days before the Great Judgement 'the holy angels shall die, and God alone shall remain alive' (para. 53). The Qur'an, however, never speaks of the death of angels. In fact it states that, on the Day of Judgement, eight angels shall bear the throne of Allah (Surah 69:17).

*f. Wives.* Marriage in the Qur'an binds a woman to one man, but it does not bind a man to one woman. Muslim men are free to have several wives (Surah 4:3) and an unlimited number of female servants (Surah 70:30). The 'Gospel of Barnabas', however, teaches the biblical idea of marriage: that marriage binds a man and a woman equally together: 'Let a man content himself therefore with the wife whom his creator has given him, and let him forget every other woman' (para. 115).

### *Its self-contradiction*

There are plenty of contradictions between the 'Gospel of Barnabas' and the Bible, and between the 'Gospel of Barnabas' and the Qur'an. But it also contradicts itself. I have already mentioned the example of Jesus described as the Christ and then rejected as the Messiah. Here is another contradiction:

*Jesus predicts his death.* In paragraph 193 the book gives its version of Jesus raising his friend Lazarus from the dead. Near the middle of the paragraph we read:

> Jesus having come to the sepulchre, where every one was weeping, said: 'Weep not, for Lazarus sleeps, and I am come to awake him.' The Pharisees said among themselves: 'Would to God that you did so sleep!' Then Jesus said: *'Mine hour is not yet come; but when it shall come I shall sleep in <u>like manner</u>, and shall be speedily awakened.'* Then Jesus said again: 'Take away the stone from the sepulchre.'

In other words, Jesus says that, just like Lazarus, 'he will die and after a few days be raised again from the dead.' How can Jesus predict this of himself when later in the 'Gospel of Barnabas' (paras. 216 & 217) it is Judas who is arrested and crucified in his place?

### Its absence in the writings of the early church teachers
Between the first and fourteenth centuries, no Christian teachers ever quoted from the 'Gospel of Barnabas'. If it had been considered authentic, surely it would have been cited many times during this long period. All the other books of Scripture are quoted many times. Had this 'Gospel' even been in existence, authentic or not, surely it would have been quoted by someone, but no one even mentioned it throughout 1,500 years of its supposed existence!

### Its absence in early Islamic writings
The 'Gospel of Barnabas' is widely used by Muslim apologists today, yet no Muslim writers referred to it before the fifteenth or sixteenth centuries. Surely they would have done so if it had existed. Many Muslim writers such as Ibn Hasm (d. 456 AH), Ibn Taimiyyah (d. 728 AH), and Hajji Khalifah (d. 1067 AH) would no doubt have used the 'Gospel of Barnabas'. But not a single person referred to it when Muslims and Christians were in heated debate between the seventh and fifteenth centuries.

### *Its rejection by the latest Muslim scholars*

There is little room for Muslims to continue believing that the 'Gospel of Barnabas' is an original Gospel which is consistent with the Qur'an and Islamic tradition. Not surprisingly, in recent years many Muslim scholars have rejected the book as a forgery. They have realized that to claim divine origin for such a book is an embarrassment to the cause of Islam.

The Arabic encyclopedia known as the simplified Arabic encyclopedia (which was supervised by famous Muslim scholars and was published in Cairo in 1965 by Dar Al-kalam [the pen house]) states on page 354:

> Barnabas' Bible is a spurious book written by a European in the fifteenth century. And in its description of the political and religious circumstances in Jerusalem during the time of the Christ were grave mistakes. It stated that Iesa proclaimed that he was not the Christ, but he came telling the glad tiding of the coming of Muhammad who will be the Christ.

No one can believe the 'Gospel of Barnabas' and the Qur'an at the same time. He who accepts this 'Gospel' can be neither a true Muslim, nor a true Christian. No wonder the late distinguished professor of Islam, Dr Abbas Mahmoud Al Aqqad, former professor at the Islamic university, Al Azhar Al Sharif, advised Muslims to stay away from this false 'Gospel'. According to the professor, and the facts of the case, the 'Gospel of Barnabas' destroys Islam as much, if not more, than it destroys Christianity (read for example his article in *Al-Akhbar* [the news] newspaper on 26 Oct. 1959).

## So who wrote the 'Barnabas Gospel'?

The great question we must ask about this book is, 'Who wrote it?' We have seen that the author was not familiar with the language, history or geography of the time of Jesus. The book includes several fourteenth-century ideas, and the manuscript evidence dates from the fifteenth century onwards. It is therefore reasonable to conclude that the 'Gospel of Barnabas' was written in the fourteenth century AD and not in the first century by a disciple of Jesus. Who, then, could have written it?

It was probably written by an apostate from Christianity. One scholar suggests that the author was a Spanish Muslim, forcibly converted to Christianity during the time of the Spanish Inquisition, who took private revenge by creating an Islamic 'Gospel'. Another scholar sees the Roman Catholic monk Fra Marino himself as the author. After converting to Islam (an act of revenge after losing the favour of Pope Sixtus V), he composed the manuscript and invented the story of its 'discovery'.

We cannot know for sure who wrote this book. What we do know is that it could not have been written by Barnabas.

## Conclusion

Above are just a few facts among many which prove how ridiculous the 'Gospel of Barnabas' really is. Anyone who is aware of its contents, yet continues to use it as a genuine Gospel account of Jesus at the expense of the Bible, must share in the guilt of the author.

This work, far from being an authentic first-century account of the facts about Jesus, is actually a late medieval fabrication. The only genuine first-century records we have of the life of Christ are found in the New Testament. The four biblical Gospels contradict the teaching of the 'Gospel of Barnabas'.

## Note

1.  Another Herod is mentioned in Luke 23:7. He reigned at the time of the death of Jesus. It was a different King Herod who reigned when Jesus was born.

# 4
# Do Christians worship three gods?

OVER THE CENTURIES, CERTAIN CHRISTIAN CONCEPTS HAVE been misunderstood. One false idea is that Christians believe in three gods. Another is that the Trinity is made up of God, Mary and Jesus.

First of all, it must be stated that Christians do not believe in three gods! The Trinity has nothing to do with *a number* of gods, but with *the nature* of the one true God.

Secondly, Mary is not God, nor is she part of God. At the time of the rise of Islam, some so-called Christians mistakenly believed Mary to be part of the Trinity. But the true followers of Jesus did not share their belief, because the Holy Word of God does not teach it. It teaches that although Mary was a good woman, she was a sinful human being, like all of us.

God wants us to know who he is. He longs for us to understand him rightly, according to what he has revealed of himself in his Holy Word. We need to learn how the teaching about the Trinity was understood by early Christians as they looked at God's Word. In this chapter, we will briefly discuss how those early Christians came to understand God as Father, Son and Holy Spirit; three persons, yet one God. Why do Christians today still insist on this teaching?

## Did early Christians believe in three gods?

No! Most early Christians were from a Jewish background. Judaism, as you know, is a monotheistic religion; that is, Jews believe that there is only one God, and that this God, Yahweh, is the God of Abraham, Isaac and Jacob. The early Christians continued to affirm their belief in this one God. They knew that the God of the Old Testament (Tawrat, Zabur, and the writings of the other prophets) is the God that Christians worship.

The early Christians lived among the polytheistic peoples of the Roman world. Most people in first-century Greek and Roman society believed in many gods. Since polytheism was all around them, Christians could have been tempted to start believing in three gods in order to try to fit in with society. But this did not happen! Christians never entertained such an idea. They continued to believe that there is only one God. Why did they do this? They did it simply because they believed the Scriptures. Let us briefly look at some evidence which makes it clear that both the Old Testament and the New Testament affirm that there is only one God.

### Old Testament support for monotheism

The Old Testament declares this truth very clearly. In fact, the opening verse of the Holy Bible reads, 'In the beginning God created the heavens and the earth' (Genesis 1:1). God created all that exists. There is not one god of the sun, one god of the moon and yet another of the stars. No, there is one God who made the stars, the moon, the sun—and everything else.

Let us consider some other Old Testament verses. Moses said, 'To you it was shown, that you might know that the LORD himself is God; there is none other besides him' (Deuteronomy 4:35). Later, Moses again declared, 'Hear, O Israel: the LORD our God, the LORD is one!' (Deuteronomy 6:4).

Solomon spoke these words, 'And may these words of mine, with which I have made supplication before the LORD, be near the LORD our God day and night, that he may maintain the cause of his servant and the cause of his people Israel, as each day may require, that all the peoples of the earth may know that the LORD is God; there is no other' (1 Kings 8:59–60). What a statement!

In another passage, God spoke through the prophet Isaiah and said, 'I am the LORD, and there is no other; there is no God besides me' (Isaiah 45:5). Again, God said in Isaiah 46:9: 'Remember the former things of old, for I am God, and there is no other; I am God, and there is none like me.'

The early Christians, then, saw clearly from the Old Testament Scriptures that there is only one God. But does the New Testament (Injil) also state this? Let us have a look at some important verses from the New Testament.

### New Testament support for monotheism

The New Testament also states clearly that there is only one God. For example, John (one of Jesus' disciples) asserts, 'And this is eternal life, that they may know you, the only true God' (John 17:3). Only God gives eternal life, and the God who does this is one.

The apostle Paul says plainly, 'Yet for us there is one God, the Father, of whom are all things, and we for him' (1 Corinthians 8:6). Writing to Christians in Rome, Paul asserts the same truth: 'Or is he the God of the Jews only? Is he not also the God of the Gentiles? Yes, of the Gentiles also, since there is one God who will justify the circumcised by faith and the uncircumcised through faith' (Romans 3:29–30). The God who brings Jews and Gentiles together through faith in Jesus Christ is one God.

When the apostle Paul wrote his first letter to his fellow worker

Timothy, he said, 'For there is one God and one mediator between God and men, the man Christ Jesus' (1 Timothy 2:5).

James, a brother of Jesus, wrote one of the books in the New Testament. It says, 'You believe that there is one God. You do well. Even the demons believe—and tremble!' (James 2:19). How sad it would be if Christians were to deny what even the demons get right!

So the early Christians, like Christians today, believed what the Old and New Testaments teach about God: that there is only one God.

## Since there is only one God, why do Christians talk about the Trinity?

The Bible *does* teach that there is only one God, but that is not all that it teaches. It also reveals truths about Jesus and the Holy Spirit. Let us see what the Old and New Testaments say about the Trinity.

### New Testament support for the Trinity

John wrote, 'In the beginning was the Word [Jesus], and the Word was with God, and the Word was God … All things were made through him, and without him nothing was made that was made' (John 1:1–3). These opening verses of John's Gospel are very profound. However, we are even more amazed when we go on to read that the Word, who is God, 'became flesh and dwelt among us, and we beheld his glory, the glory as of the only begotten of the Father, full of grace and truth' (John 1:14). We see that John talks of Jesus as both identical to God ('the Word was God') and distinguished from God ('the Word became flesh').

We must also consider the claims that Jesus made for himself. One of the most famous is found in John 8:58. He said to the Jewish religious people, 'Most assuredly, I say to you, before Abraham was, I Am.' This was an incredible thing to say! Jesus stated that he existed before Abraham lived. That was not all that Jesus meant. The people picked up stones and threw them at Jesus because they thought he was blaspheming. Why? Because when God revealed himself to Moses he said, 'I AM WHO I AM' (Exodus 3:14). By saying 'before Abraham was, I AM,' Jesus was actually claiming to be God.

The Bible is full of clear indications that Jesus is both man and God. His holiness, his sinless life, his ability to forgive sin, his infinite power and knowledge—these are all signs of his deity.

But what about the Holy Spirit? Does the Bible teach the deity of the Holy Spirit? Yes. Consider one of the many verses that show this.

The Bible tells us that, in the early church, a couple called Ananias and Sapphira sold property and gave the apostles a portion of the money they received. However, they claimed to have brought all the money. The apostle Peter was enabled by the Holy Spirit to know that they had lied. He said, 'Ananias, why has Satan filled your heart *to lie to the Holy Spirit* and keep back part of the price of the land for yourself? While it remained, was it not your own? And after it was sold, was it not in your own control? Why have you conceived this thing in your heart? *You have not lied to men but to God*' (Acts 5:3–4). So, to lie to the Holy Spirit is to lie to God. The Holy Spirit is truly God. There are many other verses which show this.

Father, Son and Holy Spirit: each is fully God; yet there is only one God. But does the Old Testament (the Tawrat, Zabur, and the writings of the other prophets) also speak of this truth? Yes, it does.

### Old Testament support for the Trinity

Old Testament believers knew that there was a plurality in the Godhead. This can be seen from the very beginning of the Bible. Genesis 1:26–27 (part of the Tawrat) reads, 'Then God said, "Let *us* make man in *our* image, according to *our* likeness" … So God created man in his own image.' The words written in italics show that God, who is one, speaks as more than one. The verse emphasizes both the unity and the plurality of God. A few pages later, we read, 'Then the LORD God said, "Behold, the man has become like one of *us*"' (Genesis 3:22). Only one God is to be found in these passages. Yet he speaks in the plural! Centuries later, a prophet called Isaiah heard God Jehovah saying, 'Whom shall I send, and who will go for *us*?' (Isaiah 6:8).

There are also many references to the Angel of the Lord in the Old

Testament, and on each occasion it is plain that God's messenger is God. Genesis 16:7–13 records how Hagar, who had run away from Abraham and Sarah, was commanded by 'the Angel of the Lord' to return. It is then made clear that it was the Lord himself who was speaking to her. She called him, 'You are the God who sees.' The one who was sent by God was God himself!

Abraham himself had a visit from the Angel of the Lord some time later. He appeared as a man, but the text clearly states that the visitor was the Lord himself (Genesis 22:11–23). Abraham recognized this and offered prayer to him.

The Old Testament also tells us that God speaks to God. King David wrote in Psalm 110:1: 'The LORD said to my Lord: "Sit at my right hand, till I make your enemies your footstool."' There are two names for God in Hebrew: Yahweh and Adonay. Here God (Yahweh is the word used) addresses someone whom David calls his 'Lord' (Adonay). The two are one. The one referred to here as Adonay is none other than Jesus Christ. Again and again we are confronted by the mysterious truth that there is multiplicity in God's unity.

So the idea of the Trinity (plurality within the unity of the Godhead) is clearly present in the Old Testament.

What can we conclude? Both the Old and the New Testaments clearly teach that there is only one God, but they also teach that the Father is God, Jesus is God, and the Holy Spirit is God. God is three, yet one. How could Christians summarize this teaching? They selected the word *Trinity* (*Tri-unity)* which means 'three one-ness'. This word has been used since the second century.

### In which sense is God both one and three?

There is one God, expressed in three persons. God is *one in nature*, but *three in person*. This is not a contradiction, even though we cannot fully understand it. There is unity and diversity.

The Father, the Son and the Holy Spirit each possess the divine nature equally, eternally, simultaneously and fully. They are not each one third of God. Each is fully God. They are not three gods, but three persons of the one Godhead. What distinguishes them is their function, their role and their relationships to each other. In unique and remarkable ways, each member of the Trinity relates to the other members, contributing to the fulfilment of the common purposes of God. It is God the Father who made a wonderful plan of salvation for mankind. It is God the Son who came to earth to fulfil the Father's plan. It is God the Holy Spirit who works in our hearts to save us. Yet the three are one.

## Conclusion

We must seek to understand who God is, but which of us can understand him fully? It is futile to try to understand the Trinity through human reason. An infinite God cannot be fully understood by finite people. He is beyond human reason. One great leader of the early church said, 'It is easier to pour the entire ocean in a little cup than to grasp the greatness of God in the human mind.' Do you agree? Then please, though the Trinity is a mystery, let us accept by faith that God, who is one, is also 'three in one'.

Friend, it is impossible to know the truth about God without studying his Word. I cannot help you to believe this mystery unless you are willing either to hear the Bible explained, or to open it for yourself. You will find helpful verses like Matthew 28:19 where Jesus commands us to go and make disciples, 'baptizing them in *the name* of the Father and of the Son and of the Holy Spirit'. Notice that he did not say 'names', but 'name'.

Since the first century, followers of Jesus have therefore come to know God as a loving heavenly Father who cares for mankind; as a redeeming Saviour who shows the way to God; and as an ever-present Spirit who gives comfort, guidance and strength. Will you trust God and come to him now?

# 5
# How can God have a Son?

'How can you Christians believe in a human god who eats, drinks and sleeps? Aren't you ashamed of yourselves?' Mosques, TV programmes and magazines tell Muslims that Christians worship a weak human god. Some Muslims therefore mock Christians and refuse to talk about this issue. Others, however, want to ask questions and discuss with an open mind. If that is true of you, then to you I direct the following series of questions.

## Where did Christians get the idea that Jesus is the Son of God?

It is not a random idea that someone thought up. It is what the Word of God says. When the angel Gabriel appeared to Mary he said, 'And behold, you will conceive in your womb and bring forth a Son, and shall call his name Jesus. He will be great, and will be called the Son of the Highest [God]' (Luke 1:31–32). Thirty years later Jesus said to a man, '"Do you believe in the Son of God?" He answered and said, "Who is he, Lord, that I may believe in him?" And Jesus said to him, "You have both seen him and it is he who is talking with you"' (John 9:35–37).

## What does 'the Son of God' really mean?

Let us think about how we use the word son (ابن). Once when I asked a friend where he was from, he replied, 'I am a son of Tunisia.' Did he mean that Tunisia had a wife who gave birth? Of course not! What he meant is that he is Tunisian and has Tunisian characteristics. So when the Bible says that Jesus is the Son of God, it means that he has the characteristics of God. Those who speak Arabic will understand the following sentence, فلان عربي ابن عرب (this man is an Arab, the son of an Arab). We use the phrase to emphasize the man's Arabic origin. He *really is* an Arab. So when the Bible says that Jesus is the Son of God, it means that he *really is* God. We also say, ابن عشر سنوات فلان (this man is a son of ten years). We mean that his age *equals* ten years. The phrase Son of God therefore indicates that Jesus is *equal to* God.

You see, the name Son of God does *not* mean that God had a wife. It does *not* mean that God married Mary who gave birth to Jesus. That would truly be a blasphemy. The meaning is far deeper. The prophets Abraham, Isaac, Moses, David and Isaiah would have understood the true meaning of the phrase 'the Son of God'.

## What did the prophets of the Old Testament say about the coming of Jesus Christ?

A prophet called Isaiah foretold Jesus' birth 700 years beforehand, saying, 'For unto us a Child is born [Jesus], unto us a *Son* is given; and the government will be upon his shoulder. And his name will be called Wonderful, Counsellor, Mighty God, everlasting Father, Prince of Peace' (Isaiah 9:6). Isaiah says that the Child 'will be born to *us*', thus affirming the humanity of Jesus. But he also writes, 'a Son will be *given* to us'. Jesus was born of a woman—he was born to us, but his birth was of divine origin—he was *given* to us.

Isaiah said that the Son who was to come would be called:

*Wonderful.* This word is generally used in Hebrew to refer to the miraculous work of God. A miracle is something that is beyond the scope of human ability. In other words, it is something only God can do.

*Counsellor.* His every instruction is wonderful. His opinions are extraordinary. His recommendations are without a fault. His advice is phenomenal. He is the only one worth listening to. Jesus is the wisdom of God. The promised Son would do things that only God can do. Just in case we are in any doubt, Isaiah tells us that this is a word he attributes to God: 'This also comes from the LORD of hosts, who is wonderful in counsel and excellent in guidance' (Isaiah 28:29).

*Mighty God.* This refers to the divinity and power of the Child to be born. This Child is the one of whom the apostle John would say 780 years later, 'In the beginning was the Word [Jesus], and the Word was with God, and *the Word was God* ... And the Word became flesh and dwelt among us, and we beheld his glory, the glory as of the only begotten of the Father, full of grace and truth' (John 1:1,14).

*Everlasting Father.* This literally means 'Father of eternity'. The rule of the promised Messiah knows no end. His government is like that of a father. In Jesus we have a love that will not let us go. George Matheson, a devout Christian who lived between 1842 and 1906, wrote about this love in a hymn that Christians sing in many churches today:

O Love that will not let me go,
I rest my weary soul in thee.
I give Thee back the life I owe,
That in Thine ocean depths its flow
May richer, fuller be.

*Prince of Peace.* Jesus is the exclusive owner of peace. He said, 'Peace I leave with you, my peace I give to you; not as the world gives do I give to you' (Injil, John 14:27). The peace that Jesus gives is a peace between God and man. Jesus offers peace to men and women through faith in him. Many people are trying to make peace, but it has already been done. God has not left it for us to do; all we have to do is to enter into it.

So, long before a baby cried in a manger in Bethlehem, the prophet said that this child would be unique. A human child, yes, but a child who was also divine. If you asked any Jewish person before the birth of Jesus, 'Who can be called the Son of God?' he or she would reply, 'Only someone who is divine—equal to God.' That is why, when Jesus claimed to be the Son of God, they accused him of blasphemy and crucified him.

### Where does the Word of God say that Jesus is God in human form?

There are many verses in the Word of God that state this fact, but here I will mention just three examples.

In his first letter to Timothy, Paul wrote, '*God was manifested in the flesh,* justified in the Spirit, seen by angels, preached among the Gentiles, believed on in the world, received up in glory' (1 Timothy 3:16). Writing to a church in Colosse (in Modern Turkey), Paul wrote, 'For in [Christ] dwells all the fullness of *the Godhead bodily*' (Colossians 2:9). Again, writing to another church, Paul said, 'Let this mind be in you which was also in Christ Jesus, who, being in the form of God, did not consider it robbery to be equal with God, but made himself of no reputation, taking the form of a bondservant, and coming in the likeness of men' (Philippians 2:5–7).

As we saw in the previous chapter, John, one of Jesus' disciples, wrote this, 'In the beginning was the Word ... and the Word was God ... And *the Word became flesh* and dwelt among us' (John 1:1, 14).

### But Jesus never calls himself the Son of God in the Bible ...

Many Muslim friends make this claim. But it is not true. Jesus called himself the Son of God many times, as the following passages prove.

One day Jesus asked his disciples a question: '"Who do you say that I am?" Simon Peter answered and said, "You are the Christ, *the Son of the living God.*" Jesus answered and said to him, "Blessed are you, Simon Bar-Jonah, for flesh and blood has not revealed this to you, but my Father who is in heaven"' (Matthew 16:15–17).

When Jesus was arrested, the religious people who hated him asked, 'Are you then *the Son of God?*' To this Jesus replied, 'You rightly say that I am' (Luke 22:70). Immediately they accused him of blasphemy and asked for his crucifixion.

In other places, Jesus spoke of God as 'my Father', making clear that he is the Son of God. He said, '…my *Father* gives you the true bread from heaven … All that the *Father* gives me will come to me, and the one who comes to me I will by no means cast out … And this is the will of him who sent me, that everyone who sees *the Son* and believes in him may have everlasting life; and I will raise him up at the last day' (John 6:32–40).

Elsewhere, Jesus said to his disciples, 'He who has seen me has seen the *Father*… Do you not believe that I am in the *Father*, and the *Father* in me?' (John 14:1–11).

On one occasion, the Jews said to Jesus, 'If you are the Christ, tell us plainly.'

'I told you, and you do not believe … I and my Father are one,' was Jesus' reply. Then the Jews picked up stones to stone him. But Jesus said to them, 'Many good works I have shown you from my Father. For which of those works do you stone me?' 'For a good work we do not stone you, but for blasphemy, and because you, being a man, make yourself God,' the Jews replied.

Jesus answered them, 'Is it not written in your law, "I said, 'You are gods'?" If he called them gods, to whom the word of God came (and the Scripture cannot be broken), do you say of him [Jesus] whom the Father sanctified and sent into the world, "You are blaspheming," because I said, "*I am the Son of God*"?' (John 10:22–36).

### Did God cease to be God when he came in the form of man?

No! When God spoke to Moses from the burning bush (Exodus 3:1–6), did he stop being God? Of course not. God cannot be limited by anything. When God revealed himself in the form of a man, he was not limited by that humanity. He continued to rule the universe. He continued to be what he always had been (God), but in Jesus, he also became what he had never previously been (man). Jesus Christ was not 50% God and 50% man. He was 100% God and 100% man: fully God and fully man. The divine person took upon himself a human nature. We really cannot understand the mystery of how this happened. But it is conceivable, certainly, that God has the power to add to himself a human nature and do it in such a way as to unite two natures in one person.

In order to illustrate this, imagine a brilliant light. Now imagine that the light is put inside a glass. Does the glass stop the light shining? No! In fact, as the light is reflected by the glass, it shines even more brightly. In a similar way, when God became man in the person of Jesus Christ, the body did not stop him being God. Jesus said, 'I am the light of the world.' God became what he had never previously been (man) but he continued to shine and to rule the universe. In this way, he revealed himself to the world *more clearly*.

### But why did God come in the likeness of men?

Why did God have to become man? What was the point? This is a very important question. It is the heart of Christianity. To know the answer, we must go back to the beginning of creation. We need to grasp what happened in the Garden of Eden.

Adam and Eve were told that the day they sinned, they would surely die. They ignored God and sinned, not by mistake, but through deliberate disobedience. Their bodies were eventually put in the grave. But, in one sense, Adam and Eve actually died the very day they sinned against God. They died spiritually. At first they had walked with God in a loving relationship. But when they disobeyed, sin formed a barrier between them and their Creator. There was an infinite gap between them and God. We call this spiritual death. It is because Adam was already spiritually dead that he died physically several hundred years later.

As a result of what happened in the Garden of Eden, all of us are born with a huge gap between us and God. By nature we are separated from God. It is our disobedience which separates us. The prophet David wrote, 'Behold, I was brought forth in iniquity, and in sin my mother conceived me' (Zabur, Psalm 51:5). Likewise, Paul the apostle said, 'For all have sinned and fall short of the glory of God' (Injil, Romans 3:23). Every man is sinful at heart; though someone may seem to be very holy outwardly, there remain sins of wrong motives, sins of the mind.

The prophet Isaiah asked the question, 'How then can we be saved?' He says, 'We are all like an unclean thing, and all our righteousnesses are like filthy rags ... and our iniquities, like the wind, have taken us away' (Isaiah 64:5–6).

What is the solution? Is there any hope? Many people try to bridge the gap by their own efforts. Some think they can get to God by being good religious people. They hope that their good deeds will outweigh their bad deeds enough to get them into paradise. But they never succeed. No one is perfect. It is not even that their contribution 'nearly but not quite' reaches God. The reality is that we fall infinitely short of the requirements. We can never reach God's standard by our own efforts. No matter how righteous we try to be, we are condemned by James 2:10 (Injil): 'For whoever shall keep the whole law, and yet stumble in one point, he is guilty of all.' Our sins can never be forgiven by striving toward self-righteousness. The gap between us and God is still there.

The question remains; what is the solution?

Once, when I was sitting quietly, I saw a troop of ants marching up and down a wall. They were trying to carry a grain of wheat to the top; but without success. The grain of wheat was too heavy. The pull of gravity was greater than their efforts! I pitied them. I wondered how I could help those hopeless ants. If I had reached down with my hand, I might have squashed some of them by mistake. They would have run away in fear. I could not help them. The only way I could have helped them was by becoming an ant, while keeping my human strength! Only that way could I help without terrifying them.

We are a bit like those ants. We can never reach God by our own efforts and good works. The gravity of our sin is too great. It is stronger than our efforts. Sin weighs heavily on our shoulders. But God pitied us. To liberate us from the tyranny of sin, he came in our likeness. He came as a man, but lived without sin. That was the main difference between him and us. Who can re-establish the broken relationship between God and man? Surely, the only one who can bridge the gap is one who is both God and man.

When Jesus died on the cross, he died as our perfect human substitute. He took the punishment that we deserve for our sin. He removed the barrier that separates us from God. But how could one man be the substitute for so many people? Since Jesus is also the divine Son of God, his sacrifice was enough to cover the sins of all those who believe in him. To sin against the infinite God is to sin infinitely and therefore to deserve infinite punishment. Left to ourselves we are lost. Only Jesus, the infinite Son of God, was able to take that infinite punishment in our place.

## What is your answer to Jesus?

I hope this has helped you to understand what the holy Word of God means by calling Jesus 'the Son of God'. I hope you now see that Christians do not blaspheme the Almighty God. I pray that God, who loves the world so much, will help you to see this issue very clearly. He wants to help you and set you free from the bondage of sin. His desire is that you will also be saved from its consequences. God is so concerned that he came to earth, taking the form of a man, so that you may know him personally and be reconciled to him. Will you receive him?

# 6

## Did Jesus really die on the cross?

THE CRUCIFIXION, DEATH AND RESURRECTION OF JESUS CHRIST are at the heart of the Christian faith. Everything a Christian believes in and hopes for revolves around Jesus' death on the cross for unworthy sinners. If it can be proven that Jesus did not die and rise from the dead, then Christianity is nothing more than a great lie which has deceived literally billions throughout the ages. The Christian is left without hope, having no assurance of salvation or of going to paradise. He remains in his sins (Bible, 1 Corinthians 15:12–19; Romans 4:25; 5:8–11).

However, there is overwhelming historical and factual evidence that Jesus died on the cross and rose again on the third day. The evidence for Christ's death is greater than that for almost any other event in the ancient world. The historicity of the gospel records has been confirmed by a multitude of New Testament manuscripts and contemporary eyewitnesses.

### The prophets foretold the death of Jesus
Seven hundred years before the time of Jesus, the prophet Isaiah foretold what the Messiah would do. He wrote, 'Surely he [Christ]

has borne our griefs and carried our sorrows; yet we esteemed him stricken, smitten by God, and afflicted. But he was wounded for our transgressions, he was bruised for our iniquities; the chastisement for our peace was upon him, and by his stripes we are healed. All we like sheep have gone astray; we have turned, every one, to his own way; and the LORD has laid on him the iniquity of us all. He was oppressed and he was afflicted, yet he opened not his mouth; he was led as a lamb to the slaughter, and as a sheep before its shearers is silent, so he opened not his mouth. He was taken from prison and from judgement, and who will declare his generation? For he was cut off from the land of the living; for the transgressions of my people he was stricken. And they made his grave with the wicked—but with the rich at his death, because he had done no violence, nor was any deceit in his mouth' (Isaiah 53:4–9).

The prophet David also spoke of the death of Jesus. 'My strength is dried up like a potsherd, and my tongue clings to my jaws; you have brought me to the dust of death. For dogs have surrounded me; the congregation of the wicked has enclosed me. They pierced my hands and my feet; I can count all my bones. They look and stare at me. They divide my garments among them, and for my clothing they cast lots' (Zabur, Psalm 22:15–18).

When we read the Gospel accounts of how Jesus actually died, we are amazed at how the prophets described everything in such detail, hundreds of years beforehand: his silence in the face of false accusations, the way he was 'slaughtered' on our behalf, his death between criminals, the fact that his body was laid in a rich man's tomb, his pierced hands and feet, the stares of the crowd. The prophets even mentioned the soldiers who gambled for his clothes!

## Secular historians accept the crucifixion

Secondly, consider that secular history confirms the crucifixion of Jesus. The second-century Greek writer, Lucian, speaks of Christ as 'the man who was crucified in Palestine because he introduced a new cult into the world'. He calls him the 'crucified sophist'. The 'letter of Mara Bar-Serapion' (ca. AD 73), housed in the British Museum, speaks of Christ's death, asking: 'What advantage did the Jews gain from executing their wise King?' There was also a Roman writer, Phlegon, who spoke of Christ's death and resurrection in his *Chronicles*, saying, 'Jesus, while alive, was of no assistance to himself, but that he arose after death, and exhibited the marks of his punishment, and showed how his hands had been pierced by nails.'

Cornelius Tacitus was the greatest historian of the Roman Empire. He wrote, 'The name Christians is derived from Christ, who was executed under the government of the procurator Pilate.'

## Early Christians believed Jesus died

The earliest Christian writers after the time of Jesus affirmed his death on the cross by crucifixion. Polycarp, a disciple of the apostle John, repeatedly referred to the death of Jesus, speaking, for example, of 'our Lord Jesus Christ, who for our sins suffered even unto death'. Ignatius (AD 30–107), a friend of Polycarp, wrote, 'And he [Jesus] really suffered and died, and rose again. Otherwise', he added, 'all his apostles who suffered for this belief, died in vain. But, (in truth) none of these sufferings were in vain; for the Lord (Jesus) was really crucified by the ungodly.'

## The Qur'an accepts Jesus' death

Ninety per cent of the time, the Muslim will immediately quote, 'They killed him not, they crucified him not, but it was likened unto them. They killed Him not knowingly, but God raised him and God is the most merciful of merciful' (Qur'an 4:157–159). In the Muslim mind, this verse says that God could never have allowed a great prophet like Jesus to be crucified by his enemies. They believe God rescued Jesus by taking him up to heaven. Muslims also believe that Judas Iscariot, who had betrayed Jesus the night before, was changed into the likeness of Christ and was crucified in his place.

But does this verse really say that Jesus did not die? What does, 'They killed Him not knowingly,' mean? We need to remember the Jews' attitude toward Christ. When Jesus was taken to the Roman governor, they did not believe he was the Messiah. They wanted to get rid of him. By saying, 'They killed Him not knowingly,' the Qur'an simply states that they killed Jesus without knowing he was the Messiah.

In fact, there are other verses in the Qur'an which say that Jesus *was* killed. The Qur'an claims that Jesus said, 'Peace unto me the day I was born, the day I died and was taken to heaven' (Qur'an, Surah Maryam 19:33).

'Behold! Allah said: "O Jesus! I will take thee to Me [*Arabic: mutawaffeeka, meaning 'I will cause you to die'*] and raise thee to Myself and clear thee [of the falsehoods] of those who blaspheme; I will make those who follow thee superior to those who reject faith, to the Day of Resurrection"' (Qur'an, Surah AL Imran 3:55; see also Surah Al-Maida 5:116,117).

These Qur'anic texts state that Jesus Christ died even though they do not say how his death took place.

## Did someone else die in Jesus' place?

Let us return to the scene of the cross and question the eyewitnesses:

1. The apostle John was so near Jesus at the time of his death that he saw blood and water flow out of Jesus' chest wound (John 19:33–37). John knew Jesus intimately and would certainly have noticed if the crucified man was somebody else!
2. If Judas or someone else was substituted, why did they not scream out that a mistake had been made?
3. How could Mary, the mother of Jesus, not see such a fraud as she stood at the foot of the cross and heard his voice speak lovingly to her? Mary was standing nearby. Nobody would know Jesus better than his own mother. Moreover, what about the two other women who stood close to the cross (John 19:25). They knew Jesus well. Surely, if someone else had appeared on the cross instead, they would have shouted, 'Hey, that's not Jesus!'

4. The centurion was a top professional in execution. He would not make such a mistake and allow anyone but the one delivered by Pontius Pilate to be crucified. That same professional executioner confessed faith in Jesus because Jesus exhibited such holiness. A sinful man like Judas could never have left such an impression on the centurion.

5. The Gospels record seven statements that Jesus made while on the cross. No one else could have said such remarkable words. For example, how could anyone other than Jesus pray, while in excruciating pain, that God would forgive his persecutors? How could such merciful and compassionate sentiments come from the lips of Judas?

6. When Nicodemus and Joseph came to take the body of Jesus down they would have known immediately if it was someone else.

7. The criminal executed alongside Jesus would not have called on him for salvation, and received salvation, if it was just another sinner there on that cross beside him.

Besides, what would you think of God if for thousands of years he promised that Jesus would come and die for the sins of the world, and then, at the last moment, when Jesus was about to be put on the cross, he took him alive and changed someone else into the image of Christ? Does this description fit God? Not only would this make God out to be a liar, but there would have been no provision for man's sin! Jesus was the only sacrifice sufficient for man's salvation.

## Jesus really died!

Jesus' injuries made death unavoidable. He had no sleep the night before he was crucified; he was brutally beaten and whipped, and he collapsed while carrying his cross. This prelude to the crucifixion alone was life-draining. So let us be clear that Jesus *was* dead—without any shadow of a doubt. He was certified as dead by the centurion in charge of the execution squad. Pilate, the governor, double-checked to make sure Jesus was dead before he gave the body to be buried. 'Pilate marvelled that he was already dead; and summoning the centurion, he asked him if he had been dead for some time. So when he found out from the centurion, he granted the body to Joseph' (Mark 15:44–45). The crowning proof of Jesus' death is that when a spear was thrust into his side under his heart in order to make sure he was dead, out came what an eyewitness called blood and water (John 19:34). Obviously the scientific explanation of this was unknown to men of those days, but the diagnosis is clear. Dark blood and light serum came from the body of Jesus, and the separation of clot from serum in the blood is the strongest medical proof that the patient is dead. So do not be taken in by any of the 'swoon' theories which imagine that Jesus was not quite dead but recovered in the cool of the tomb! He was most certainly dead.

## Why was Jesus' death necessary?

Yet why did Christ need to die? Could he not have saved us without dying? Man had broken God's law and the penalty was death: physical and spiritual. 'The wages of sin is death' (Romans 6:23). How could Jesus Christ deliver us without meeting our full penalty?

Death is man's big problem. If anyone were to save us, he would have to resolve this problem. He would have to conquer death. He would have to restore our broken relationship with God.

When Adam and Eve disobeyed, God immediately promised to send them a Saviour. Through that Saviour's suffering, people would be saved (Genesis 3:14–15; Isaiah 53). In fact, the Bible says that 'it pleased the Lord' to offer Christ as a sacrifice for man's sin (Isaiah 53:10).

A judge sat in the courtroom, wearing his judicial robe. A young girl stood before him. She had been charged with driving without a licence and speeding down the highway. The penalty for these charges was two thousand pounds. He pointed his finger at her and asked, *'Are you guilty or not?'* to which she answered, *'Yes, Your Honour, but I cannot afford to pay the penalty.'* The judge simply said, *'You must pay,'* and then closed court. He stepped down from the bench, took off his robe and gave the girl two thousand pounds. Why? Because he was her father. He could not dishonour his name by letting her go free, but he was also merciful and loving and could not bear to see her put in jail because of her inability to pay. The only solution, therefore, was for him to pay the penalty himself.

In the same way, Christ has paid the penalty for our sin. God is holy. He hates sin, so he cannot simply close his eyes to our disobedience. Because he is a just and fair God, he must punish sinners. Death is our penalty; spiritual death, physical death, then ultimately, eternal separation from God. No mere man could ever pay that penalty for us. But in his mercy, God decided to pay the penalty himself so that we can go free. Jesus Christ, being equal with God, took off his robe of heavenly glory and came down to earth as a man. On the cross, he was punished for our sins. The justice and mercy of God came together, and both were satisfied.

Without Jesus' death there would have been *no way* for us to escape God's punishment for our sin.

### What is the evidence that Jesus' death was sufficient for man's salvation?

The evidence is the resurrection of Jesus from the dead. By raising Jesus from the dead, God declared to the world that he had accepted Jesus' sacrifice on our behalf.

If Jesus had remained in the grave, we would have seen that he was just another sinful human being like us. His death would have been worthless. He would have died for his own sins, not ours. The resurrection shows that death could not keep its hold on Jesus. It shows that God, the Judge, considered our penalty to have been paid. Our sins had been dealt with. Jesus broke the death barrier.

Anyone who has said goodbye to a departed loved one at a graveside knows that death is a formidable enemy. Yet for Christians facing death, there is the certainty of eternal life beyond the grave. This certainty comes from the knowledge that Jesus Christ overcame death and its sting. Jesus did this through his triumphant resurrection. 'Death is swallowed up in victory. O Death, where is your sting?' (1 Corinthians 15:54–55).

## If Jesus died on the cross, and if Jesus is God, does that mean that God died on the cross?

God is Spirit. In the original Hebrew language, Spirit is *roh*. From this word, the word *rihe* is taken, which means 'the air'. We can say, therefore, that God's Spirit is like the air in the atmosphere. Air is everywhere. Though you cannot see it, you know it is present: you can feel it, you breathe it, even though it has no colour or shape. Similarly, the Spirit of God is present everywhere.

An empty bottle does not contain any liquid, but you know that it is full of air. The air inside the bottle has taken the shape of the bottle, even though air has no shape. The characteristics of the air inside the bottle are similar to the characteristics of the air outside the bottle. The fact that there is air inside the bottle does not mean that there is no air outside the bottle! Now, if you were to take the bottle and smash it against a wall, it would break into hundreds of pieces. It would be shattered. Could we say that the air inside the bottle would also be shattered? No. Only the form that contained the air would have been shattered.

A similar thing took place when God, who is Spirit, dwelt among us in the body of Jesus Christ. God took the likeness of man. That did not mean that he no longer existed elsewhere. Like the air when it filled the bottle, God still existed everywhere. Furthermore, Jesus' crucifixion did not mean that God was killed, but rather that the human body which contained the Spirit of God was killed. God always lived, even during the three days when Jesus was dead in the tomb.

## Conclusion

Jesus really died! The New Testament explains that it was not out of weakness that God allowed Jesus to be crucified. Jesus said, 'Therefore my Father loves me, because I lay down my life that I may take it again. No one takes it from me, but I lay it down of myself. I have power to lay it down, and I have power to take it again' (John 10:17–18). In a moment Jesus could have summoned a legion of angels to rescue him. But he chose not to because he knew that through his death God's plan to save sinners would be accomplished.

By raising Jesus from the dead, God not only vindicated Jesus and revealed his true identity, he also destroyed the power of death for all who trust in him.

# 7

# Is Muhammad mentioned in the Bible?

'WE MUSLIMS BELIEVE THAT JESUS WAS A PROPHET. WHY don't Christians recognize Muhammad as a prophet?'

'If we recognized Muhammad as a prophet, we would be Muslims, not Christians.'

'Yes, but your Bible speaks of Muhammad. Jesus himself predicted his coming.'

'Here is a Bible, can you tell me where it mentions Muhammad?'

'I don't know, but the Qur'an says he's predicted in your Bible!'

For many years, Muslim apologists have tried to find predictions of Muhammad's coming in the Tawrat, Zabur and Injil, but to no avail. This chapter will examine three main passages that are referred to as supposed predictions of the coming of Muhammad.

## Is Muhammad mentioned in the Tawrat?

Muslims refer to Deuteronomy 18:18 (Tawrat) where God says to

Moses: 'I will raise up for them a prophet like you from among their brethren, and will put my words in his mouth, and he shall speak to them all that I command him.' Muslims believe that this prophet was Muhammad. Abraham had two sons: Ishmael and Isaac. It is assumed that '*their brethren*' refers to the Ishmaelites, and since Muhammad was descended from Ishmael, he must be the prophet. However, a brief look at the background of the prophecy reveals that it was not the Ishmaelites who were in mind.

### Who is God referring to with the words 'them' and 'their'?

My father used to work as an Arabic teacher and he often helped me with my Arabic homework. Whenever I asked him about the meaning of a word he would tell me to read the whole sentence or paragraph. I usually discovered the meaning myself just by reading the word in context! This is exactly what we must do when we read the Bible. We cannot just pick a word or paragraph out of context and make it say what we want. We must look at the whole context.

This prophecy is part of a discourse in which God gave Moses certain directions about the way the people of Israel (especially the Levite tribe) should conduct themselves once they reached the promised land. The first two verses of the chapter clearly reveal who God was referring to as 'their brethren': 'The priests, the Levites—all the tribe of Levi—shall have no part nor inheritance with *Israel*; they shall eat the offerings of the LORD made by fire, and his portion. Therefore they shall have no inheritance among *their brethren*; the LORD is their inheritance, as he said to them' (Deuteronomy 18:1–2).

It is clear that God is talking about the Levites. 'Their brethren' are the other tribes of Israel. Moses states that God will raise up a prophet like himself from among the Jews, from among their brethren. The prophet will be a Jew. Muhammad was not a Jew. He was born an Arab. The Arab people are not one of the tribes of Israel. So Muhammad was not Moses' brother.

Who then fits the description of a prophet like Moses? Jesus Christ does. The New Testament (Injil) as a whole makes it plain that Moses' prophecy in Deuteronomy chapter 18 was fulfilled in Jesus Christ of Nazareth. Jesus himself said, 'If you believed Moses, you would believe me; for he wrote about me' (John 5:46–47). He never said, 'Moses wrote about Muhammad'.

In the Gospel of John 1:45, we read words spoken by the apostle Philip: 'We have found him of whom Moses in the law, and also the prophets, wrote—Jesus of Nazareth.' Jesus was born of the tribe of Judah through Mary. Thus he was a Jew, an Israelite like Moses.

In Acts chapter 7 of the New Testament, Stephen says clearly that Moses foretold Jesus Christ. The apostle Peter declares the same thing in Acts 3:19–23: 'Repent therefore and be converted, that your sins may be blotted out, so that times of refreshing may come from the presence of the Lord, and that he may send Jesus Christ, who was preached to you before, whom heaven must receive until the times of restoration of all things, which God has spoken by the mouth of all his holy prophets since the world began. For Moses truly said to the fathers, "The LORD your God will raise up for you a prophet like me from your brethren. Him you shall hear in all things, whatever he says to you. And it shall be that every soul who will not hear that Prophet shall be utterly destroyed from among the people."'

## Are there predictions of Muhammad in any other part of the Old Testament?

A second verse that Muslim apologists refer to in support of their claims is Isaiah 29:12: 'Then the book is delivered to one who is illiterate, saying, "Read this, please." And he says, "I am not literate."' Muslims insist that: (a) the book referred to in this verse is the Qur'an; (b) the one to whom the book is delivered is Muhammad; and (c) the one who orders Muhammad to read the book is the angel Gabriel. They suggest that Muhammad fits the description of this individual, since he was illiterate when Gabriel revealed the words of Allah to him.

Once again we must not take the words out of their context. To understand the context of the verse, we must remember that Isaiah (who lived in the eighth century BC) is known as the 'messianic prophet' because he prophesied so many details about Jesus—not Muhammad. In Isaiah 29 God pronounces judgements on Judah for her sins at that time (i.e. 702 BC).

The passage indicates that within a year, the great Assyrian king Sennacherib would lay siege to Jerusalem (v. 3). Jerusalem (called 'Ariel') would be attacked by her enemies and punished for her sins against God, and then those enemies in turn would receive their just deserts (vv. 4–8).

God's people were in deliberate spiritual blindness. To them the Bible was a closed book, and Judah's false prophets were not helping the situation (vv. 9–10). Notice that Isaiah then describes the unwillingness of the people of his day to heed the truth, by comparing them to a *literate* person who is told to read something, but refuses, excusing himself by saying the document is sealed (v. 11). Isaiah then likens the people to an *illiterate* person, who excuses himself by saying he cannot read (v. 12).

The point is that the people of Isaiah's day refused to pay attention to God's Holy Word as spoken through his prophets. They did not want it! Verses 13–16 explain that because of their closed minds, they will suffer for their rejection of God's Word when the Assyrians arrive to besiege the city. But, as usual, God reveals a better day when people will listen (vv. 17–18).

Having examined the context, it is evident that these verses have nothing to do with Muhammad!

### Is there a prophecy about Muhammad in the Injil?

'According to your Bible, didn't Jesus speak of a prophet to come whom he called the Helper? This is obviously a prophecy about Muhammad.'

Muslims often make this claim. After all, the Qur'an declares, 'And when Jesus son of Mary said: O Children of Israel! Lo! I am the messenger of Allah unto you, confirming that which was (revealed) before me in the Torah, and bringing good tidings of a messenger who cometh after me, whose name is Ahmad (the Praised One)' (Qur'an 61:6).

Muslims appeal to verses like John 14:16–20, where Jesus says, 'And I will pray the Father, and he will give you another Helper.' Most Muslims quote only the first half of this verse, and then shut the Bible! If Jesus stopped at this point, one could speculate about the identity of this Helper. But Jesus clearly identifies him by continuing, 'that he [the Helper] may abide with you for ever—the Spirit of truth, whom the world cannot receive, because it neither sees him nor knows him; but you know him, for he dwells with you and will be in you'.

From the earliest centuries of Islam, Muslim scholars have endeavoured to prove that this Helper was Muhammad, the prophet of Islam. It is argued that the Greek word *parakletos,* which is translated 'Helper', should be *pareklutos* or 'praised one', meaning Ahmad or Muhammad. This is proof, they say, that the biblical text has been changed! However, any knowledgeable scholar in the field will tell you that there is no evidence at all for this 'corruption'. All of the Greek manuscripts in existence, which predate Muhammad, say *parakletos,* not *paraklutos.* There are more than seventy Greek manuscripts of the New Testament in existence today, dating from before the time of Muhammad, and not one of them uses the word *paraklutos*! All use the word *parakletos.* In fact the word *paraklutos* does not appear anywhere in the Bible!

Let us now look at the specific details of the arrival and identity of this *parakletos,* 'Helper', and see if they fit Muhammad.

### 'He will give you another Helper'

Even if, as Muslims claim, the original word was *paraklutos,* the sentence would read, 'He will give you another praised one.' It makes no sense and is completely out of context. What Jesus is saying here is this: 'I have been your Helper, Counsellor, Comforter. I still have many things to teach you, but I will send you another Helper like me.'

### 'He will give you another Helper—the Spirit of Truth'

The one obvious fact that emerges is that the Helper is a Spirit. Has Muhammad ever been called the Spirit of Truth?

### 'That he may abide with you for ever'

In no sense was Muhammad ever with Jesus' disciples, let alone permanently. Muhammad was born in the seventh century after Christ. He lived only sixty-two years and then died. He did not live with his companions for ever, did he? His body was buried in Medina. But Jesus said that the promised Helper would be with his disciples for ever. The one referred to cannot possibly be Muhammad.

### 'The Spirit of Truth, whom the world cannot … see'

According to this prophecy, the world cannot receive the Helper because it cannot see him. Thousands of people saw Muhammad during his lifetime, for he was visible. The *invisible* Helper cannot be the *visible* Muhammad.

### 'You know him, for he dwells with you'

Jesus is clearly talking about someone with whom the disciples were familiar. Was Muhammad known to them? Of course not. He was born more than five hundred years later.

### 'He dwells … in you'

The Helper was to be *in* the disciples. How could the Helper be Muhammad? Muhammad was a flesh and blood person who is no longer alive. Muhammad is not *in* Jesus' followers and never will be.

What can we conclude? Was Muhammad alive at the time of Jesus' apostles? No. Was Muhammad ever called the 'Spirit of Truth'? No. Did Muhammad live with the apostles for ever? No. Did Muhammad live inside the apostles? No. So this prophecy cannot be a reference to Muhammad.

Who is it about? The Bible states the truth in the following verses. 'But the Helper, *the Holy Spirit*, whom the Father will send in my name, he will teach you all things, and bring to your remembrance all things that I said to you' (John 14:26). It is certain, then, that the Helper is the Holy Spirit (Ruh Al-Kudus) of God.

The fulfilment of this prophecy occurred within a matter of days. Only fifty days after the resurrection of Jesus, the disciples received the Helper on the day of Pentecost. Jesus had told them to wait in Jerusalem until the Holy Spirit, the Helper, should come (Acts 1:4–8). The Holy Spirit came upon them while they were all together, praying in the city. 'And they were all filled with the Holy Spirit' (Acts 2:3–4). The Holy Spirit was *with* the disciples in the person of Jesus while Jesus was still on earth, and the Holy Spirit was *in* the disciples' hearts from the day of Pentecost and for ever.

The Helper is indeed the Holy Spirit of the living God. We all need him to open our eyes so that we can see who Jesus is and what he has done for sinners like us. The Helper is only given to those who believe the gospel: that Jesus died for our sins and rose again. This is what makes someone a Christian. Only those who believe and trust in Jesus will receive the Helper. You can receive the Holy Spirit today by genuinely accepting Jesus into your life and acknowledging him as your Saviour.

## Conclusion

All of these verses (and others that Muslims refer to) can be understood with a little study and consideration of context. Those who apply these passages to Muhammad demonstrate that they have a superficial understanding of the Bible. The truth is available for anyone who is willing to examine it. Searching for the truth requires effort, yet it can be done. As Jesus said, 'You shall know the truth, and the truth shall make you free' (John 8:32).

Muslims and Christians alike agree that Christ's coming was often predicted in the Old Testament (Tawrat + Zabur + the writings of the prophets). If God had intended to send another prophet who would be far greater than Jesus Christ, surely we would find predictions about him too. None are to be found. There was no need for another prophet to come after Jesus. When Adam and Eve sinned against God, man's relationship with God was broken. However, because God is full of compassion and mercy, he promised to send a Saviour (not just a prophet) to rescue the world. People try to escape God's judgement by relying entirely on their good works, but, as we have already seen, God's Word says we can never please God by how good our lives are. We are not able to make amends for our sins. We are hopeless. But God decided to have mercy on us. He knew that there was only one way to resolve our problem: to deal with it himself. We did not need someone who was just a great prophet. We needed a Saviour who came to take away our sins.

All the prophets—Noah, Abraham, Moses, David and others— remind us of God's promise. They prophesied and described the Saviour who would come. Later, when the prophet John the Baptist saw Jesus, he said that Jesus was the promised Saviour, the fulfilment of God's pledge to Adam and Eve. If the promised Saviour has come, why should we look for someone else?

Jesus said, 'I am the way, the truth, and the life. No one comes to the Father except through me' (John 14:6). Notice that Jesus did not say, 'I am one way among many that will be shown to you in the future.' No, he said that he is the only way to paradise. Jesus was able to make this claim because he died on the cross to take the punishment that our sins deserve. That is how our sins are dealt with. It was not Buddha, Muhammad or any other person who died on the cross to pay for our sins. The Holy Book, the Bible, tells us: 'Nor is there salvation in any other, for there is no other name under heaven given among men by which we must be saved' (Acts 4:12). There is no other way to God and salvation except through Jesus. Jesus' sacrifice on the cross is sufficient. We do not need another prophet or another name. One greater than a prophet, a Saviour, has come. Only Jesus can restore our relationship with God. Only Jesus can forgive us our sin and give us eternal life. Only he can make us sure that we will go to paradise.

# 8

# Sure of going to paradise?

'I WISH I COULD BE SURE!' MY FRIEND SAID. 'BUT THERE'S NO WAY for me to know if I'm going to paradise or hell. I try to live a decent life, but I'll have to wait until the Day of Judgement to see where God will put me ... right now, I don't know where that will be.'

'Wouldn't it be nice', I asked, 'to be sure that if you died you'd go straight to paradise?'

'No one at all can be sure of going to paradise,' he answered. 'Do you know anyone who's sure?'

'Yes, I know someone,' I replied. 'I Amos'

'How dare you say that?!' he shouted.

And then he left. Perhaps you would have said the same thing!

## I had the wrong key!
My family and I were looking forward to spending a few days at the home of a friend by the coast about 150 miles away. He had delivered a key to us a few days earlier, saying, 'Our winter home is unoccupied.

You and your family may go out there and take a little vacation as my guests.'

We found the house and, with keen anticipation, went to the door and put the key into the lock. It would not fit. We tried the back door. No success. Our friend had given us the wrong key, and all of his good intentions did not get us into the house. We spent the night in a hotel.

The right key is even more important in the spiritual realm. If you hope to get into paradise, you ought to be very sure that your key will unlock the door to eternal life.

Our friend's mistake cost us only a little disappointment and the price of accommodation for one night. But what will it cost the person who depends on the wrong key to get him into paradise? The cost is too great to be calculated. 'For what will it profit a man if he gains the whole world, and loses his own soul? Or what will a man give in exchange for his soul?' (Mark 8:36–37).

Consider the following story about a wicked man who went to paradise.

### An evil man who went to paradise!

It was 9 o'clock in the morning when they nailed Jesus to a cross. Two thieves were crucified at the same time. The Bible tells us that Jesus was in the middle, with one thief on his right and the other on his left. These two thieves were probably members of a violent gang led by a man called Barabbas. If so, they were merciless criminals who cut throats, robbed houses and violated women. They were greedy, cruel and unkind.

From 9.00am till 12 noon, people walked by the three crosses, throwing up insults and mockery into Jesus' face. Both thieves did the same. Yet, by 12 o'clock, Jesus had promised that one of them would go to paradise. Something extraordinary must have happened during those three hours!

The thief was suddenly overwhelmed by a sense of God and the guilt of his own sin. He realized that the person he was insulting (Jesus) was the pure and sinless King. So he prayed to Jesus saying, 'Lord, remember me when you come into your kingdom.' Here we see that this thief had faith. Jesus Christ answered him and said, 'Assuredly, I say to you, *today* you will be with me in *paradise*' (Injil, Luke 23:42–43). In Greek, the word 'assuredly' means '*it is fixed*' and '*it cannot be changed*'. Jesus told this man (an evil thief, remember) that he would go to paradise, *that day*. And we do not read that Jesus said anything else to him at all. The man did not need to hear anything else, did he?

| TODAY: | What speed! |
| WITH ME: | What company! |
| IN PARADISE: | What happiness! |

Just before Jesus died, he cried out, 'It is finished!' (Injil, John 19:30). What was finished? Jesus had finished taking the punishment that we deserve for our sin. He suffered, body and soul, in place of all those who trust in him. But now his work was accomplished, finished. When Jesus died and went immediately to his Father's presence in paradise, he went in the company of that thief.

What wonderful good news this is! It means that all your sin can be forgiven. It means that you can be with Christ in paradise the moment you die.

### But how can I get there?
Jesus is the way. He said, 'I am the way, the truth, and the life. No one comes to the Father except through me' (Injil, John 14:6). Think about that thief. Was he promised paradise because of his good works? Did he have time to put right his past life? Well, he would be dead by 3.00pm! He would have no time in six hours to put his life right even if he could get off the cross. Did he give to the poor? Did he fast? Don't get me wrong, these are good things to do, *but they are not the door into paradise*.

- Do you have to be a special person to go to paradise? NO!
- Do you have to be in a special place? NO!

- Do you have to say special words? NO!
- Do you have to have special accomplishments? NO!

So who goes to heaven? Christ does! In his own right. Because he is perfect. And everybody who is clinging to him, trusting in what he did for us on the cross, goes with him. That is the only condition.

## If those who trust in Jesus are sure of going to heaven, don't they just live however they want?

Many people ask this question: 'If someone knows they are going to paradise, can they just do whatever they want, yet still be saved?'

We find the answer in the Bible: 'What shall we say then? Shall we continue in sin that grace may abound? Certainly not! How shall we [Christians] who died to sin live any longer in it?' (Injil, Romans 6:1–2).

Jesus' death and resurrection were the focus of God's perfect plan to save sinners *and set them free from slavery to sin.* The Bible says that the moment a person sincerely puts his trust in Jesus Christ and receives him as Saviour and Lord, three great things happen.

*1. He is saved (or set free) from the penalty of sin.* God forgives all of that person's sin. God is just and fair. He must punish all the wrong things we do. But Jesus took the punishment that we deserve. The price has been paid. 'There is therefore now no condemnation to those who are in Christ Jesus' (Injil, Romans 8:1).

*2. He is saved (or delivered) from the power of sin.* God gives that person a new heart. Then he comes to live in it through his Holy Spirit. The person starts to look at life in a radically new way. He now hates sin and loves what is true and right. 'Therefore, if anyone is in Christ, he is a new creation; old things have passed away; behold, all things have become new' (2 Corinthians 5:17). The Bible also says, 'The fruit of the Spirit is love, joy, peace, longsuffering, kindness, goodness, faithfulness, gentleness, self-control...' (Galatians 5:22–23). These things will start to characterize that person's life because he has been made new and clean on the inside.

*3. He shall be saved (or freed) from the presence of sin.* One day Jesus Christ will come back to judge the world. On that day, he will punish those who rejected him, but those who trusted in him and followed his commands will be rewarded. He will deliver them from the presence of sin.

So anyone who says, 'I am forgiven and can do anything I like,' cannot be a real Christian, since there is no evidence that the Holy Spirit is working in his life.

## You can be sure of going to paradise

Yes, you can be sure of going to paradise. Your eternal destiny is not decided by your good or bad works. Entrance into paradise is a free gift from God, received through faith in Jesus Christ. The Bible says, 'For by grace you have been saved through faith, and that not of yourselves; it is the gift of God, not of works, lest anyone should boast' (Injil, Ephesians 2:8–9).

### Will you be there?

My friend, God has given us a way to be saved from slavery to sin and from his judgement; a way to paradise. In paradise there is no sin, so there will be none of the sad and bad things that make life on earth so tough. This is what Jesus says to everyone who believes in him: 'In my Father's house are many mansions; if it were not so, I would have told you. I go there to prepare a place for you. And if I go and prepare a place for you, I will come again and receive you to myself; that where I am, there you may be also' (John 14:2–3). You can see why no Christian is afraid of the Day of Judgement! In fact, Christians look forward to Jesus' return. On that day he will send to hell all those who refused his free offer of salvation, but he will take his people home to paradise.

Jesus lived the blameless life that you and I should have lived, and he succeeded where you and I have failed. People mocked him. They crucified him. Yet all this fulfilled God's plan to rescue us from sin.

Will you confess your guilt to God and give your heart and life to Jesus Christ? Once you do that (like that thief), God promises to give you a new heart—and to reserve a place for you in paradise!

# 9
# What about the ungodly life of some 'Christians'?

'Look at how immoral Western society has become! Is this what Christianity has done to the West?' Some people think that Christianity has caused the problems. Perhaps that is what you think, too. Let me urge you to consider the following points.

## Genuine Christians are grieved by the immorality they see in Western society

The ungodly lifestyle of most people in Western society is heartbreaking. It has caused a great deal of pain for the true followers of Jesus Christ. Immorality is everywhere: idolatry, drug and alcohol abuse, girls going around half-dressed, divorces, infidelity, fornication, family breakdown, the rejection of marriage—the list goes on!

Many Muslims wrongly think that Christians encourage an immoral lifestyle. This idea is completely false. God is the origin and founder of Christianity. The Tawrat, Zabur and Injil have always warned people to be careful not to grieve God by living an ungodly life.

Muslims are often surprised when they read the Bible and see how seriously it speaks about moral and ethical issues. Take the example of man-woman relationshiPsalm The Bible is absolutely against any sexual relationship outside marriage. In fact, Jesus said that if a man simply looks at a woman and desires her in his heart, he commits adultery. The thought itself is wrong. It is as if he has actually slept with her. Jesus taught husbands and wives to be loving and faithful to each other; he taught parents to bring up their children to obey God and respect his commands; he taught children to obey their parents. Jesus even taught people to love their enemies! I could give many more examples.

The truth is that the moral state of society is getting worse and worse because people refuse to listen to God's Word. They want to live without God. They want to be the gods of their own lives. So many people have no idea what the Word of God (the Bible) is all about! No wonder, then, that they live in a way that displeases God. The problem is that Muslims think that every Westerner is a Christian. This is not true.

## Not every European is a Christian

I used to think that everyone born in the West is a Christian. I thought that, just as everyone born in a Muslim family is automatically Muslim, so every Westerner is Christian by birth. When I first came to Europe I was shocked to find out that this is not true. I discovered that many people in Europe don't believe in God. They want to live without him!

The Bible does not teach that someone who is born in a Western country is automatically a Christian. Being born in France, England, or the USA *cannot* make you a Christian. No one is a Christian by birth. You have to become a Christian. If someone becomes a Christian it means that there is a time in his life when God opens his eyes to see the awfulness of the wrong things he has done against his Creator. We call this 'conviction of sin'. This leads him to see what Jesus did for him when he died on the cross. He sees clearly that God dealt with his sins by sending Jesus to die as a substitute for sinners. The person then turns away from his sins (repents) and receives Jesus as his Lord and Saviour. It is at this point that the person becomes a Christian: a follower of Jesus. It is not because he is European, but because he has accepted and embraced Jesus. Nationality has nothing to do with it. Jesus came as the Saviour of the world; that is, the Saviour for people of every tribe and nation.

## Not everybody who claims to be a Christian is a real Christian

Many people call themselves 'Christians' simply because they occasionally attend church, or because they are not Muslim, Buddhist, Hindu, or Spiritist, or because they were born to Christian parents, even though they themselves have never received Jesus Christ as their Saviour. They are 'Christian' in name only. They have never experienced a transformation in their lives. They have never allowed Jesus to forgive their sins and make them into new people. Therefore they keep on doing detestable things even though they call themselves Christians.

There are others who, under the cloak of Christianity, seem to be pious and righteous. On the outside they look good, but on the inside they are full of hypocrisy and wickedness. Jesus opposed people like this and told them plainly, 'You are like whitewashed tombs which indeed appear beautiful outwardly, but inside are full of dead men's bones and all uncleanness. Even so you also outwardly appear righteous to men, but inside you are full of hypocrisy and lawlessness' (Matthew 23:27–28). Jesus Christ also said, 'Not everyone who says to me, "Lord, Lord," shall enter the kingdom of heaven, but he who does the will of my Father in heaven. Many will say to me in that day [the Day of Judgement], "Lord, Lord, have we not prophesied in your name, cast out demons in your name, and done many wonders in your name?" And then I will declare to them, "I never knew you; depart from me, you who practise lawlessness!"' (Matthew 7:21–23). Indeed,

'Man looks at the outward appearance, but the LORD looks at the heart' (1 Samuel 16:7).

## How do true Christians live?

God's Holy Word gives us many examples of how true followers of Jesus Christ live. When the disciples had received the promised Holy Spirit (the Helper), the apostle Peter stood up and spoke to people about Jesus. This is how they responded:

> Then those who gladly received his word were baptized; and that day about three thousand souls were added to them. And they continued steadfastly in the apostles' doctrine and fellowship, in the breaking of bread, and in prayers … Now all who believed were together, and had all things in common, and sold their possessions and goods, and divided them among all, as anyone had need. So continuing daily with one accord in the temple, and breaking bread from house to house, they ate their food with gladness and simplicity of heart, praising God and having favour with all the people. And the Lord added to the church daily those who were being saved                    (Acts 2:41–47).

These verses describe the lives of the first Christian believers. Today, true followers of Jesus seek to live in the same way. They do these things not to try to earn salvation, but because God has already saved them and changed their lives. In other words, these things are marks that someone has become a true follower of Jesus Christ.

### Baptism

In the Bible, baptism follows conversion. It is a symbol to show that the person's sins have been washed away. As someone is plunged under the water and brought back up again, believers are also reminded that they have left their sinful life behind. It is as if they have died, and are being raised up again to live a life that pleases God.

### Doctrine

When people become followers of Jesus, they long to understand more of God's Holy Word, the Bible, and to put what they read into practice. In this passage we see that the believers were devoted to the study of what the apostles taught. True Christians love the Bible. They love to read it and to hear people explaining it to them. They have been delivered from the power of sin in their lives, so they are able to put what they learn into practice.

### Fellowship

The word 'fellowship' has been translated from the Greek word *koinonia*, which means 'the sharing of things in common'. Christians come from all walks of life. Some of them have university degrees, while others have had virtually no education. There are Christians from all sorts of racial, cultural and social backgrounds. Some are young, some are old. All of these diverse people come together because they have ONE thing in common—Jesus Christ. He is the basis of their fellowship. A true follower of Jesus wants to be part of that fellowship.

### Prayers

Christians love to talk to God, their heavenly Father, in prayer. They pray together and on their own. They worship God and thank him for all he has done for them. They confess their sins. They bring their troubles to him and they pray for other people.

### Providing for the needy

In the passage we also see that the early Christians sold their possessions in order to help those who were in need. Jesus often made statements such as, 'By this all will know that you are my disciples, if you have love for one another' (John 13:35). Elsewhere, the Injil says, 'Let us not love in word or in tongue, but in deed and in truth' (1 John 3:18). Love must be very practical. Christians should show love through meeting the needs of others.

### Worshipping God

Followers of Jesus meet together regularly to praise and worship God, adoring him for who he is and for what he has done for them.

## Conclusion

It is true that some people who profess to be Christians are hypocrites, but it is not true that all Christians are hypocrites. There are many genuine, committed Christians who have been forgiven and changed by Jesus Christ. They seek to live their lives by Jesus' standards. The Holy Spirit who dwells in them helps them to live in a way that pleases God. They love Jesus and follow his commands to be holy and to live righteously.

# 10

# Why am I a Christian?

What we have discussed is not empty speculation. Millions of people all over the world have experienced the reality of it for themselves. Here is a personal account of how Jesus saved someone from North Africa. My hope is that, through this interview, you too will come to see the importance of having your sins forgiven through Jesus Christ.

**You were born into a Muslim family.**
**Did you actively practise Islam?**
Yes, very much so. My parents are practising Muslims and I was brought up to know and follow the principles of Islam. I observed the five pillars, though I never had the opportunity to go on pilgrimage. I prayed five times a day and fasted during Ramadan every year. My father encouraged me to memorize many chapters (Surahs) of the Qur'an. I frequently led prayer times for my fellow students when I was at university.

**How old were you when you started going to the mosque?**
I started going to the mosque when I was very small. My dad was keen to take me with him, especially on Fridays. I also went to Islamic classes every day during the school holidays. I still remember the fakih

(Qur'anic teacher) tapping us on the head with his long stick! My mum often prepared breakfasts for us to take and share with the others.

## Tell us a bit about what your parents taught you.

Every Muslim hopes to go to paradise. That was my dream too. But how could I get there? My parents taught me that I had to work hard and to live as a good Muslim.

## Can you explain that in more detail?

As a Muslim I believed that there was an angel on each side of me. The angel on the right recorded all my good works; the one on the left recorded all my bad works. On the Day of Judgement, my works would be weighed in a balance. My hope was that my good works would outweigh my bad ones. For that to happen I had to pray a lot, fast, help the poor and so on.

## Does that mean that an earnest Muslim can be sure of going to paradise?

No Muslim is sure of going to paradise.

## Why?

They must do their best and wait for the Day of Judgement. Even if their good works outweigh their bad works, it will still be up to Allah to choose whether to let them into paradise.

## What is the Muslim view of paradise?

Qur'anic passages regarding paradise are dominated by descriptions of sensual delights waiting for the faithful. Paradise in Islam is a place where every man will have many beautiful women to serve him. Wine will no longer be forbidden. There will be a nice river … You can understand why I longed for paradise! According to traditions of Muhammad's journey from Mecca to Jerusalem, and afterwards to the heavens, Allah is absent from all but the seventh of the Islamic heavens.[1]

## I thought wine is forbidden by Islam!

Yes, but it will not be forbidden in paradise.

## How can Allah forbid things on earth but allow them in paradise?

It is a reward for Muslims who exercise self-control in their life! Some Muslims believe that the heavenly wine does not make one drunk.

## Now you are a Christian, how do you think of paradise?

Paradise is so amazing that no one can fully imagine it. One thing I know is that in paradise I will see God face to face and have a perfect relationship with him. I will live eternally in his presence. There will be no sin there. I will love and worship God with all my heart, soul and strength. That's why I look forward to it.

## Before you became a Christian, did you fear that you would not go to paradise?

Oh yes. Though I tried hard to be a good Muslim, I never had peace of mind. In fact I was always afraid of death. To be honest, I had no idea where I would end up.

## Did you ever doubt Islam?

I remember one incident that occurred when I was fifteen. I was in an Islamic lesson at the college where my dad worked. That day we were studying a passage from the Qur'an which speaks of the Day of Judgement. It says that Allah will choose certain Muslims to go to paradise, but reject other Muslims. I remember feeling that if that was the case, I could have no certainty of going to paradise. I protested, 'But it's not fair! If I'm doing my best to please Allah, why won't he promise me paradise?' The teacher was very angry. He told my dad what had happened!

## What happened afterwards?

I had to do more prayers and fast for a few days so that Allah would forgive me for doubting.

## What did you know about Christianity at that time?

Nothing. All I knew was what I had seen in films. Actually, I thought that every Westerner was a Christian by birth.

## Do you still think that?

When I understood what it really means to be a Christian, I was shocked to realize that, in fact, only a small percentage of the Western population are genuine Christians.

## What do you mean by 'genuine Christians'?

No one is born a Christian. People become Christians. A Christian is someone who believes that Jesus died for his or her sins. He believes that he can be saved through what Jesus did on the cross. A Christian trusts Jesus and receives him as Saviour and Lord. So not every Westerner is a Christian. In fact, sadly, most people in the West live as if God doesn't exist. That's why there is so much immorality.

## What was your view of God when you were Muslim?

I had always believed that the universe had a divine Creator. Allah was that Creator. I believed that Allah was all-powerful, all-knowing and present everywhere. But I also believed that he was unapproachable, incomprehensible, and that we should not even attempt to describe him with human language. I believed that Allah revealed himself in the pages of the Qur'an, and to a certain extent through creation. But Allah was hidden, inaccessible. He could never be known in a personal way.

## What about Jesus and the Bible?

Jesus is respected by Islam as a great prophet, but only a great prophet. He is called the Messiah. I believed in his virgin birth and his miracles, but to say that he died on the cross was blasphemous. I believed that someone else took Jesus' place on the cross, while he was taken up to heaven. I also believed that the Torah, the Psalms and the Gospels, as well as the Qur'an, are revelations from God. However, Christians and Jews are accused of distorting and falsifying their Scriptures. Consequently I did not believe that the Bible as it is today is a true revelation from God.

## Were you looking for God, or was that not something that concerned you?

I had always believed in a divine Creator. What I was really looking for was peace with God and the assurance of a place in paradise. I tried hard to please Allah by my own works—to be a good Muslim. But I felt that I could never succeed. The heart of the problem was the problem of my heart! I was often afraid of death, knowing that I had nothing good to bring before God.

## Tell us how you heard about Christ

My brother was the first person to tell me about Jesus. He moved to Europe and gave his life to Christ eight years before me. Like most North African immigrants, he returned to North Africa for the summer holidays. One year he spoke to me about Jesus. Since I reacted angrily, the only thing he could do was leave me an Arabic New Testament (Injil) before he went back to Europe. I remember that day well! At first I didn't realize that the book he had given me was a Bible. He phoned me later to tell me what it was.

## How did you react?

I was very afraid at first! I ran and hid it from my parents. But although I kept the book, I didn't read it. A year later, I went to Europe to continue my postgraduate studies. There I started studying the Arabic Bible. I also met other Christians who helped me to understand the Word of God. Seven months later God opened my eyes and I trusted in Jesus Christ for myself.

## What changed your mind about reading the Bible?

Before I went to Europe, I had trouble getting a Visa to travel there. My brother often emailed to encourage me. He also said that his Christian friends were praying for me. I was amazed that people who had never met me were concerned enough to pray! Where did they get that love for others? Surely there must be something good in their Injil. I wanted to find out what their book said. But that wasn't my only motive in reading it. I also hoped to find faults in the Injil so that I could argue with my brother!

## What did you discover in the Bible?

I knew I could never be good enough to merit paradise. When I started reading the Bible I found that it told me exactly that! I read verses like 'There is none righteous, no, not one' (Romans 3:10). It told me that I could never be good enough to go to heaven. Left to myself, I am without hope, because I am a sinner. But it also told me that there was someone who was sinless. He never did anything wrong at all. He alone was pleasing to God in every way.

## Who was that person?

Jesus Christ. As a perfect man he lived the life that I should have lived. He died the death which I deserve. He died in my place because that was the only way for me to escape God's anger and judgement. He bore the wrath of God so that I won't have to. For the first time I could see the sure way to heaven.

## Was there anything else about the Bible that struck you?

I was very surprised to discover that the Bible includes the Tawrat, Zabur, the writings of the prophets, and the Injil! I thought that Christians only have the Injil (the New Testament). There was something else that amazed me: the Bible says that we can know God personally through Jesus Christ. That was a completely new thought to me. I could have a personal relationship with God! Me, a poor sinner!

## What is your view of God now?

The God of the Bible, in whom I now place all my confidence, is a God who is holy, just, trustworthy, faithful, honest and gracious. I believe in a God who is love; an approachable God who can be known personally. He has revealed himself in the Bible and in the person of the Lord Jesus Christ.

## How would you describe your first experiences of the Christian life?

There is no moment more joyful than when you first know that you have been saved. I remember how I was beforehand, and I know how I am now, and I see that I am a different person. I have peace deep in my soul now. It's wonderful to know that all my sins—past, present and future—have been forgiven through Christ's death on the cross.

## Can you share a moment of great joy that you have spent with Jesus?

I had been hearing the gospel and studying the Bible for seven months before I gave my life to Jesus Christ. Although I was convinced that the message was true, I was afraid to submit to it. People said that I should pray. But I didn't really know who I should pray to! Was it possible for me to pray to any God other than Allah?! One night I prayed a little prayer, saying, 'Jesus, if you are the true God, help me to give my life to you. Take away the obstacles in my heart. Allah, if you are the true God, please forgive me for my doubts. If you are the true God, I will serve you with more zeal than ever before.' The next day I woke up with the assurance that Jesus had heard my prayer.

## Was it all rosy afterwards?

Unfortunately, no! What would my family and friends say? Of course, the devil often tried to attack me with doubts about what I had done in giving my life to Christ. 'Can't you see the danger of what you are doing? Don't you understand the consequences of your decision? Is this really the way to reward your parents for all the support they've given you over the years?' These questions and many others came into my head time after time.

## How did your family react?

A year after my conversion, I went back to North Africa to see them and tell them about my conversion. First I tried to speak to my mother and my two sisters. Once they realized what I was saying, my oldest

sister stood up angrily and called me a Jew. My mother started to cry.
She asked me to go back to Europe straightaway because she was afraid
that my father might try to harm me physically if he heard the news. I
went back to Europe without telling my father, but he found out later
and cut off all contact with me. I continued to write to them once a
month, but I never received a reply.

### Why did they reject you?

A Muslim who becomes a Christian is seen as an apostate, a traitor
who deserves punishment. For a Muslim family, it is shameful for a
family member to become a Christian. They also thought that it would
make me forget my parents, my family and my culture. They thought I
would start getting drunk and living an immoral lifestyle.

### Why did your family think that?

They did not know what the Bible teaches. They believed that every
Westerner is a Christian, and that the immorality in Western countries
is caused by Christianity! There is widespread confusion about the
West and Christianity. The Holy Bible is actually against all forms of
evil and impurity. Later, my parents were very surprised to see how
seriously the Bible talks about moral issues.

### What helped you to overcome these difficulties?

Prayer! One of my Christian friends prayed regularly with me, and
God answered our prayers in wonderful ways. I began to have financial
problems because I had depended on my parents' support for the
completion of my studies. So when I became a Christian my source
of money was cut off. I really didn't know what to do. But God kindly
provided a way for me to support myself. A school asked me to give
private tutoring to pupils on Saturdays. After two years my parents
contacted me again and I now have a good relationship with them.

### A word of encouragement for those who are in the same situation?

Perhaps you are convinced that the message of the Bible is true, but you have not yet given your life to Christ. Maybe you fear the consequences that could follow your conversion. Perhaps you fear the reaction of your friends and family. Remember one serious thing: on the Day of Judgement, when Christ will be the Judge, you will face him alone. Your family and friends will not be there. What will you say to him? The Lord is ready to receive you. Will you let him into your heart?

## Note

1.   http://www.sunnahonline.com/ilm/aqeedah/0039.htm#3.

# Conclusion

J ESUS IS INDEED THE PRINCE OF PEACE. HE IS THE SOURCE OF REAL peace: the peace of God. This peace comes from knowing that your sins are forgiven and you will go to paradise. It is a peace that sustains you through the difficulties and frustrations of life. The Bible says that you must be at peace *with* God through the death and resurrection of Jesus, before you can know the peace *of* God. When Jesus died on the cross, he reconciled sinners to God. He took the wrath of God against our sin upon himself, so that those who believe in him will escape judgement.

The most important thing in life is to make sure that you are at peace with God. This cannot happen by performing good works or trying to live a good religious life. No! The Holy Word of God tells us that it is only possible through faith in the Lord Jesus Christ and his sacrifice on the cross.

After reading through these questions and answers, you may still have questions about your eternal salvation. Perhaps you still doubt and resist God's plan and his free offer to save you from your sin. I urge you to trust in Jesus Christ the Messiah. Perhaps you were given this book by a friend or maybe you came across it by accident. It was no accident! God has given you an opportunity to learn about Jesus his

Son, the Saviour. If you look to him, you will receive the forgiveness of your sins and everlasting life in paradise with God.

## How can I receive Jesus?

You can receive Jesus into your life now, by talking to him sincerely in prayer. Open your heart to him, acknowledge and confess your sins. Ask God to wash you from your sins by the blood that Jesus spilt on the cross. God forgives those who humble themselves before him in this way. He is perfectly aware of all that is in your heart, so it is useless trying to hide anything. God wants you to turn to him.

I encourage you to take God's Holy Word very seriously. Don't let anything stop you putting right your relationship with God.

- Acknowledge that the Lord Jesus is the Son of God.
- Admit that you have done many things which are against his will. Tell him that you are a sinner and turn away from all the bad things you have done. Ask the Lord Jesus to forgive your sins.
- Open your heart to Jesus as your Saviour and Lord. Acknowledge his right to reign in your life, by submitting to the commandments in his Word, the Bible. And ask him to make you into the person he wants you to be.

The Lord is ready to adopt you as his child and to welcome you into his family. He is ready to transform your life. The Bible promises, 'as many as received him, to them he gave the right to become children of God, to those who believe in his name' (Injil, John 1:12).

# Glossary of Arabic words

| | |
|---|---|
| 'abd | servant |
| Adam | Adam |
| Ahlu Al Kitab | the people of the book: Jews and Christians |
| Bismillah | in the name of Allah |
| Daoud | David |
| Hadith | Traditions |
| 'ibn | son of |
| Imam | leader of a mosque |
| Injil | the Gospels, the New Testament |
| Isa | name of Jesus in the Qur'an |
| Islam | religion of Islam, submission, surrender (to Allah) |
| Moussa | Moses |
| Muhammad | prophet of Islam; sometimes spelt Mohammed |
| Muslim | follower of Islam |
| nabi | prophet |
| Qur'an | Book of revelation to Muhammad; sometimes spelt Koran |
| Rab | Lord |
| ruh | spirit |
| Ruh Al-Kudus | Holy Spirit |
| Salam | peace, used as greeting |

| Surah | chapter in the Qur'an |
| Tawrat | Old Testament law, the first five books of the Bible |

| yahoodee | Jew |
| Zabur | Psalms |

Muslim greeting: Assalamou Alaikoum (God's peace to you)

Reply: Wa Alaikoom Asalam (and to you peace)

## Note

As this glossary has been transcribed from Arabic script, the Roman script spelling will vary.

# Bibliography

**Chapman Colin**, *Cross and Crescent—Responding to the Challenge of Islam*, 1995, IVP, Downers Grove, United States of America.

**Geisler, N.L. and Saleeb, A.** *Answering Islam: The Crescent in the Light of the Cross,* 1993, Baker Books, Michigan, United States of America.

**Gilchrist John**, *Facing the Muslim Challenge: A Handbook of Christian-Muslim Apologetics*, 2002, Life Challenge Africa, Claremont/Cape Town, Rep. of South Africa.

**Ragg, L. & L.**, *The Gospel of Barabbas*, 1907, Clarendon Press, Oxford, United Kingdom.

### Testimonies
**Steven Masood**, *Into the light: a young Muslim's search for the truth*, 1986, Kingsway Publication Ltd, Eastbourne, East Sussex, BN23 6NT.

**David Zeidan**, *The Fifth Pillar*, 1993, Piquant/AWM, Carlisle, United Kingdom.

If you would like to receive further information or receive free
Christian literature, please contact us.

If you wish to make further study of the Christian faith,
correspondence courses
in English, Arabic and French are available at:

M.E.C. Word of Hope Ministries
22 New Street,
Rochdale,
England
OL16 3PG

www.word-of-hope.net
E-mail: contact@word-of-hope.net